SIR, YOU HAVE BREAST CANCER!

HARVEY I SINGER

ISBN: 1484186362
ISBN 13: 9781484186367

FORWARD

In 2008 I was diagnosed with Male Breast Cancer. Until that day, I, like most men, never thought this would be possible. How can a man get breast cancer?

We all have a fear, to some extent, of cancer. Just the hearing the word "CANCER and YOU" in the same sentence causes most of us to tremble and fear the worst. The world knows that the scientific scholars and doctors have made tremendous strides over the past few decades in the war on cancer. But the facts remain that we really have so much further to go. I recall asking my attending breast cancer oncologist why she would choose to go into a field of medical practice where every day she has the potential to "lose a patient". She is a brilliant woman. She could have practiced any type of medicine she wanted. "Why would she choose this field?" I also recall how her response was the antithesis of what I expected and probably what anyone would have expected.

It was not because she wanted to "help" all of those afflicted. It had nothing to do with the humanity of it, at all. She didn't say "it's my life's work to help people get through this disease and keep them around for their families". Nope, not a word of that was uttered.

It was about the SCIENCE!

"It's the challenge" she told me. "It's the fact that I come to work every day and look for an answer. An answer as to why we have so much breast cancer in our society and how hard it is to wrap our hands around it", she stated to me. I was blown away. I never thought that this would be the driving force of my doctor. After all, don't we want or think that our doctors are there just to help us get better?

All cancer patients are virtual Guinea Pigs for the next group of patients that follow. Every surgery and every chemo treatment are trials of some sort that the medical community documents and tests again.

If you survive and live on and you go into one column and if you die you go into another. No doctor, oncologist, scientist or drug company has the answer. Everyone is just taking their best shot based on your predecessors. It is truly a guessing game. It is a game that has the ultimate consequence and one that has the potential to make or ruin the rest of time that you have here on earth.

What I learned most through the process is that you better become as informed about your specific cancer as possible in order to make the best possible decisions. If you just rely and trust your doctor you may or may not like your outcome. Cancer doesn't follow any direct route map. Every cancer and each person are different, and every person reacts differently to the same medications. Our bodies are all different and some of us can fight off cancer cells and others can't. You have to be your own advocate and you better understand every aspect of your disease in order to make the best decisions.

This is what became so frustrating to me. Here I am a guy, with a "woman's" disease. They have made so many great strides with woman's breast cancer but they knew almost nothing about treating men with the same disease. Breast cancer is a hormonally driven disease. Men and women produce different hormones at different levels but because they know so little about men with breast cancer, they just treat you like a woman.

While I was doing as much due-diligence as possible to learn about my breast cancer, I found so little information pertaining to me, a "man"! Hours upon hours of internet searching where you can virtually find anything, produced very little information of substance. The more I researched the more frustrated I became. Most of what I was able to uncover were some small stories or small organizations from the families paying tribute to the man in their lives. Their husband or father, some man who they had loved and had died from the disease. It was very un-nerving!

I vowed NOT to become "just another statistic" and that I would find a way to beat my breast cancer. I promised myself that when I did beat this "fucking disease" that I would find a way to help the next guy who had to deal with it. I would find a way to give the next man just a little more information than I was able to obtain.

When you are fighting a life threatening illness, we all tend to make "deals" with God or promise to do something if we are spared. It's just human nature. Inevitably what happens is when and if you do overcome your illness, then you just go back to your normal life.

I began to pen these pages while going through chemotherapy after a mastectomy that removed my left breast. I needed a way to keep my mind working, a distraction, and keep it away from the fears and all the "what ifs". I made a dent during those four months of "Chemo-Hell" as I reverted back to a somewhat normal life, if you can call being shuffled from one test to another and sitting for days waiting on the outcomes of each test a normal life. At least I was able to go back to doing my complete job function and traveling for business once again.

I ultimately shelved the book for a couple of years as I fell back into a normal work routine.

In 2012 I finally gave in to some Psychotherapy, something I had fought against for the past three years after my first ordeal. I thought I could handle it all, like most "tough guys", but I couldn't! It was during therapy that I was encouraged to go back to my writings and complete the story I had set out to tell, the story of a "Man going through a Woman's disease".

I didn't want to write a medical memoir or a story of this doctor, or that surgery, or what chemo medications I had been utilizing. I had read enough of those types of books. I wanted to enlighten, inform and interject some laughter as I examined my past 57 years on this earth. My therapist had brought out a lot of the suppressed feelings, memories, times of my youth and the frivolity of my life and she encouraged me to engage the readers with all my personal being. The following pages were the culmination of not only the past four plus years as a cancer survivor, but a comprehensive look back at my life and what lead up to my fight against my cancer.

PERSONAL DISCLAIMER:

Every event, action and account in this book and on the pages that follow
is an accurate depiction and recount of my life's experience. Every word is
truthful to the best of my recollection.
I have changed the names for all of the doctors involved in my personal
medical history to protect their privacy, according to legal standards.
I have also changed the names of my personal friends, acquaintances and
business related personnel.
The names of my immediate family have remained.

TABLE OF CONTENTS

Chapter 1

THE BEGINNING/ PHILLY BOYZ

At 2:55pm on Wednesday October 8, 2008, my phone rang. As I looked down at the Caller I.D. and viewed the screen that said "RESTRICTED", I knew my life, as I had known it, was about to change FOREVER!

As I answered the phone, with great hesitance, the Doctor of Radiology on the other end said, "Mr. Singer?"

"Yes?" I responded.

"I have your biopsy results".

"SIR, YOU HAVE BREAST CANCER!"

You would think that hearing those words on the other end of a phone would immediately have some demonstrative and hysterical effect. It didn't. Mostly they did not because the words the doctor was saying to me were expected and anticipated. I KNEW THEY WERE COMING!

For the 30 hours after physically going through the biopsy and awaiting the official call, I knew what the results were going to be. In fact, I knew that I had breast cancer four days earlier after leaving my primary care physician's office and heading immediately to an imaging center to have a mammogram and ultra sound on the lump I had discovered just a few days earlier.

That Friday, I walked cautiously into my primary physician's office to meet with a physician assistant, as my official doctor, I was informed, was no longer affiliated with the practice. I told her that I had noticed a slight physical / visual appearance change in my left nipple about two months before. I didn't pay too much attention to it, as it looked like my 54 year old body was falling flabby all over and was just wrinkling the nipple area with some excess fat. I did notice some soreness around the area of my left nipple, but attributed this to an irritation from a Sabona magnetic bracelet one of my friends encouraged me to wear a couple of months back, during a golf outing. Murray claimed that this bracelet would help my back pain, knee pain, shoulder aches etc. He said," You never take it off. Shower with it. Play golf with it. Just wear it all the time".

As I showered with it on my right wrist, I noticed that when I washed under my left arm pit, the bracelet would rub up against my nipple and scratch or irritate it. To me this made perfect sense for the feeling of this irritation.

As a guy, you're always looking to blame something else for your pain or change in appearance and never face up to the possibility of another reality. The reality that it could be something more, something bad!

The weekend before this visit to my doctor's office had been one of the best weekends of my life. It was our annual "Philly Boyz" Weekend. One weekend every year since 1995 when a group of guys who were friends growing up in Philadelphia through the 1970's, get together to relive some of the good high times and frivolity of our youth.

I'm not exactly sure how "Philly Boyz" evolved but it has become the most anticipated weekend of the year for a bunch of Northeast Philadelphia alums who come together for a weekend to attend an Eagles game, play some golf and go crazy as we did in high school and while attending college at Temple University.

It started with six of us just meeting up for a game against the arch enemy Cowboys and has evolved into so much more with so many more people involved. We would wait for the release of the NFL schedule which normally comes out in late April or so. As soon as the schedule is released, I would scour the dates and cross reference those dates for several options for that Fall's, Philly Boyz event. I'm not sure exactly how or when I became the "CEO for Life" as one of the Boyz has bestowed upon me, but I think it was because I was always the first one to view the dates and circulate the Emails proposing several date options to the group.

Finding a perfect date is NOT as easy as you may think. Because we are predominately a Jewish group, the first dates needing to be excluded are the High Holy Days of Rosh Hashanah and Yom Kippur. Next, we also have to consider a date early enough to insure we had the best chance of having decent weather, since the golf outing has become almost as important as the Eagles game itself.

The third date I always look for is one that happens before the start of the NBA season as one of our founding Philly Boyz members, Jay, has worked for the Philadelphia 76ers for the past 15 years. And lastly, I would look for a GOOD GAME! For years, we always booked the weekend the Cowboys came to Philadelphia. The hated Cowboys! What could be better than finishing up Philly Boyz weekend

"The Philly Boyz" still remains!

Once I selected a date or two that accounted for all of the other known factors possibly affecting that date, I would circulate the Email and wait for the responses. And boy, did I have responses! Trying to please 10-12 guys with one date and with everyone's family involvements is never easy. The Emails of complaints, disdain, and sarcasm prove that fact every year.

In most cases we look for a home game in Philadelphia. We still have the bulk of our group residing in or around the Philadelphia area. But many outsiders are involved as well. Craig, one of our founding and most important members (since he has his family access to at least six game season tickets) lives in a Chicago suburb as does another founding member Murray. I reside in Upstate New York (Rochester area). Tony (our token Goyum) lives in the Albany, NY area. Philadelphia offers us, not only easy travel access for the bulk of the group, but also the added pleasure of preying on Atlantic City the day before the game for both golf and for a Saturday evening extravaganza. Since most of us grew up in the Philly area, we spent many of our "wilder" days through college, etc. at the Jersey shore. This was long before gambling was legalized in the beach town of Atlantic City, NJ, but believe me, it never stifled our partying or the good times that we had back in those days.

When the NFL schedule was released back in the spring of 08 and my annual "WHAT DATE WOULD WORK" for Philly Boyz 08 was disseminated, the two Chicago Boyz, immediately came forward to offer a suggestion," Let's move Philly Boyz to Chicago this year", they stated!

As the schedule showed, the Eagles were playing the Chicago Bears for a Sunday Night, Nationally televised NBC event, September 28th. PERFECT! We were going to hold our annual Phlly Boyz reunion and party in the windy city. What a weekend this was going to be!

Normally I get the task of coordinating and putting all of the key details together for this annual event. This year, Craig and Murray said, "We'll take it off your hands and you can take the year off! You just need to show up"!

Ok, that worked for me.

Craig and Murray arranged everything. From the unbelievable golf outing at one of the most prestigious golf courses around, to a chartered 30 foot

Sea Ray trip across the lake, down the Chicago River docking right outside of Soldier Field, to all the dinner arrangements and food for the tail gate party on the boat.

Tailgating on a boat docked right below Soldier Field is an experience every sports fan should have. I never realized that about 200 or so boats do this for every Chicago Bears home game, at least the ones that are still in nice weather.

I had been noticing that the "soreness" around my left nipple was becoming more prominent. True, I was being more active, swinging ever harder, with my "terrible golf swing" that has always been noted by most of my friends. Certainly all of these factors were contributing to the fact that I was having more discomfort. It had to be. What else could it be?

It was September 28th. Sunday morning. Game Day! Although the game wasn't to kick off until 7:00 PM central time, we left our selective hotels and other places of weekend housing to conjoin together at Craig's Deerfield, IL, home.

The golf outing on Saturday was spectacular. The weather couldn't have been more perfect. 72 degrees, sunny with a light breeze. The partying was fairly normal for a Philly Boyz weekend. Howard had his Buda Bag, filled with Bacardi Rum. Alphonse and I had our bottle of Don Julio Anejo. Cigars flowed like Legos at an eight year olds' birthday party. The golfing itself, as usual, took a back seat. Sure some of the guys can play and play well. Most of the group is made up of more casual golfers. Then there's Howard who fakes it all together. He's strictly there for the social aspect of the golf outing. Howie prefers to be in his own cart, so he can gallivant around from group to group, maybe playing a hole, maybe not. He'd offer a "shot" out of his Buda bag, or stop and smoke a cigar with that group. After golf, Murray begged us to drive over an hour each way to experience some special hot dog place called Super-Dawg, known only to Chicagoans. It wasn't worth the drive and it wasn't really that special!

After retreating back to our hotels and some to Murray's house, and a quick nap, we met up for a nice dinner in downtown Highland Park. We dined at a small local establishment that allowed us to have more interest in harassing the female waitresses than on the dinner itself. Howard and I work in the world of restaurants and hospitality and deal with outstanding professional chefs every day. We experience plenty of great meals for a living. This dinner, as most Philly Boyz meals, has nothing to do with the food itself. It was about enjoying the company and dining together with the Boyz.

After a short drive back to" Craig's Bat Cave" for a few more pops and smokes and plenty of games of blow darts, pool or just sitting in the barber's chair, we found a way to drive ourselves back to our hotels for the night. We were all pretty well spent anyway.

We began arriving at Craig's house on Sunday around 10:30 AM and hanging out in the driveway, all of us dressed in our beloved Eagle's gear. McNabb, # 5 Jerseys abound. I preferred the #36 of Brian Westbrook. We had plenty of back up clothing for the long day ahead on the water and to survive that evening's Chicago night weather.

One thing about this group of grown 50 something men is that we are all extremely close. Not just close friends and in some cases relatives. No, I'm talking VERY CLOSE. Dave, the largest guy in our group began a few years prior to start saying "Hello and Goodbye" by kissing each other. Before we have always hugged each other and on special occasions a kiss on the cheek between two Boyz this close was not abnormal. But Dave decided that kissing each other, "ON THE LIPS" was just as proper and really expressed how close, this group of guys really were. Most of the guys were never that comfortable with this, but because it was Dave, we never really said anything and we all kind of went along with it. Dave's a fairly large man. 6'4" 250lb and played linebacker in high school and for Temple University, but he is by everyone's account the sweetest man you will ever meet. He is very intelligent and never has a bad word for anyone. (Except when he's criticizing Donovan McNabb, Andy Reid or anything or anybody who is politically conservative).

Dave married my closest female cousin, Cindy. Cindy and I are four months to the day apart and we lived directly across the small Philadelphia row home street, until I was 13. We went all through elementary, junior high, and high school together. We spent almost every summer very close together in the Chelsea district of Atlantic City, usually on the same street or sometimes in the same sea shore house. One year our families even shared the same house. That was a total disaster. My mom and Aunt Lil, (Cindy's mom) fought almost every day. It didn't matter what the fight was about, it just mattered that they needed to argue about something. Like if the Jersey tomatoes my mom bought were already too soft or whether I left my toys or baseballs lying around.

My father and Cindy's mother were brother and sister and were the only siblings of their family. When our house burnt to the ground from a gas infused fire three weeks before my Bar Mitzvah, I sat and watched everything my parents owned, and that I knew, perish, from Aunt Lil's bedroom window, some 25 steps away.

Cindy and Dave met in Atlantic City several years later and they were married. She was by far the first of any of my friends of that era to get married. Obviously, Dave instantly became part of the family, part of the group. As the years passed, and to this day, I am closer to Dave than I am with my own blood cousin, but the two of us are still very close.

Dave is almost totally bald with an earring and resembles MR. CLEAN to many outsiders. He has a large pronounced mustache that "tickles" when you kiss him hello. I love him dearly, but never got passed that feeling of his mustache when we kissed.

My brother Jeff had an amazing Bar Mitzvah celebration. He is almost three years my elder. I was really looking forward to having this gigantic party with my friends and 200 of my parents' relatives and friends of whom I knew maybe 15% of them in total. Either way it was going to be a great party. The Jewish faith and the celebration of Bar Mitzvah, the coming of age from a boy to a man goes back thousands of years. Somehow, in the mid-1960's it had taken on this "life of its own" where my parents had to put on this totally elaborate event. Large banquet rooms were catered by expensive kosher caterers and a full nine piece orchestra.

It was a Sunday morning around 10:00 AM, a typical Sunday morning in our small row home in the Oxford Circle section of Northeast Philadelphia.

I was up and left the bedroom I shared with my brother Jeff and was in the small room playing a game of knuckles with my sister Vicki in her room.

We heard this loud "BANG", but went right back to playing our card game and laughed as we thought that Jeff had fallen out bed. Suddenly Seymour, my dad, came bursting into Vicki's room and asked us "what broke"? Vicki and I both answered in unison that "Jeff fell out of bed". That's when Seymour left in a hurry saying "Jeff's been downstairs for almost an hour". We didn't think much of it, but about 5 minutes later my dad came barreling back up the stairs shouting at the top of his lungs, "GET THE HELL OUT OF THE HOUSE! THE HOUSE IS ON FIRE"!

Vicki and I ran down the stairs along with our beloved French poodle, Jacque and straight out of the front door across the street to Aunt Lil and Uncle Joe's house, still in our pajamas.

It took what seemed like hours but really was only about 15 minutes for the fire department to show. By this time our home was completely engulfed in flames and because the gas heater had exploded in the basement, the house had no chance. Neither did the two neighbor's homes on either side of us since they were row homes and attached to ours.

The entire neighborhood was now outside watching as every possession my parents owned was being attacked by the flames and black smoke. Some of my friends came by to view the spectacle and told me later that they thought that I had lit a smoke bomb. I actually had done that a couple of years earlier not knowing how much "smoke there was in a smoke bomb". I think I'm still sore from the "belt" that Seymour used on me that day.

While we watched everything perish from Aunt Lil's bedroom, at 13 years of age, I had no idea of the devastation and turmoil this fire would cause in our lives. After a couple of days we were able to get back into the house. There was a giant hole from the basement right through the roof where you could see the sky. Almost everything was gone or charred to a crisp. What was interesting was that my parents had a small box in the corner of our dining room. The box had housed my Bar Mitzvah invitations and was where they had kept the RSVP's from the guests who were invited. The outside of the box was blackened but when we opened the box, "everything inside was intact". Not a mark on them.

My "big event" was reduced to a small luncheon following the Bar Mitzvah services. My parents had no idea how they were going to replace our house or how much money they actually lost in the fire. My dad always claimed that he would "make it up to me". He didn't but I understood as I got older the consequences of that fire. We eventually moved to a new house further northeast and out of Oxford Circle. My parents couldn't go back to that house but it was eventually rebuilt and sold to another family. I will never forget that "SMELL" of burnt and charred furniture and rugs.

That Sunday morning as we were meeting and shucking it up with Eagles chants and all of the great feelings that go along with every Philly Boyz weekend, an old friend of Craig's, a guy named "G" as we call him, pulled up to join us for the day. G isn't really a regular Philly Boyz member, but has partied with us in Atlantic City in the past and being a native Chicagoan and one of Craig's closest friends, he was in for today's boat trip and game.

I know G pretty well and have spent more than a few nights, golf outings with him through Craig, so when I saw him in the driveway that morning, a nice big hug was in order. Hell, we are the Philly Boyz and this is what we do!

Little did I know then and certainly totally unaware to G, that his HUG, was about to SAVE my life! That hug would also change my life as I had known it for the past 54 years and 57 days!

What happened when G came up to me and planted that great big bear hug "hello" on me was the first time I realized that I did in fact have a problem! I had hugged all of my Boyz that weekend. I had felt numerous times the irritation and soreness surrounding my left nipple. I had seen the slight fold of skin over my nipple and the slight indentation. None of it registered too high up on my HEALTH RICHTER SCALE.

THIS HUG DID!

When G hugged me I immediately felt this sharp, knife like pain that shot through my entire left chest! It was unlike any pain, soreness or anything else I had felt or associated with my left chest before. It wasn't subtle. It wasn't unclear. It screamed to my mind. "YOU HAVE A PROBLEM!"

My day and Philly Boyz-Eagles weekend continued on. But throughout the entire day's events, the boat trip, the partying, the unbelievable trip down the Chicago River, the food on the boat and the game itself, (the Eagles lost when we couldn't convert a first and goal from the Bear's two yard line to win the game) my mind consistently went back to the fact that I HAD A PROBLEM in my chest. I just didn't know exactly what the problem was, but I knew it was something of concern.

The pain eased up after an hour or so, but the soreness and the reminder of that hug persisted. It never went away and my mind certainly wasn't going to let it go away. I had to find out what was wrong.

We finished the weekend and once again another successful and memorable Philly Boyz weekend came to a close. Because the game ended so late on Sunday evening, we all caught flights back home, early on Monday morning.

I arrived home on Monday and immediately went into my office to catch up on the week's coming events. As the Director of Sales for a major hospitality uniform company, one of my responsibilities was to oversee my sales Account Executives that work on the east coast and help them to increase their sales numbers. I travel extensively. Sometimes I travel far too much as I am readily available to assist any salesperson with a major presentation for a sales opportunity.

The next day I was scheduled to fly into New York City to attend a National Autism Culinary Awareness Fundraising Event, (Autism Speaks) utilizing some of New York's finest Executive Chefs. Our company sponsored the event by creating and donating all of the chef's jackets being worn that evening. This would be a fabulous experience with unbelievable food for me and my New York City account executive.

I woke up very early Tuesday morning. I hadn't slept well since feeling the sharp pain two days earlier. My wife was still sound asleep next to me so I didn't want to get up and risk disturbing her this early in the morning. It was about 5:30AM.

I was awake and lying there in bed, still wondering what that pain might have been, I began poking and prodding the area around my left nipple. Suddenly, I felt something that didn't seem to belong. I quickly moved my hands to the right and began poking and prodding the area around my right nipple. I wanted to find the same obscure small gland or bump that I "thought" I had felt on my left side. Back and forth I went for about 10 minutes. "Is it the same here"?

Suddenly, I broke into a COLD SWEAT! That small lump, directly below and a little to the side of my left nipple, was NOT ON THE RIGHT SIDE! I remember my heart racing, sweating and thinking, "WHAT THE FUCK IS THIS"?

My wife, Donna, woke up about 30 minutes later. As usual she jumped into the shower. As she tended to her hair and the other normal rituals that 50-something women go through every morning before going off to work, I followed her and went into the shower.

At this point, I still said nothing to her about this small lump or gland or whatever it was, but it was still front and center in my thoughts. As I showered, I once again began feeling that area with great concern.

I finished my shower and as I stood next to Donna in front of our sinks, I said to her, "feel this" and pointed to my left nipple area. She looked at me a little strange when I explained, "I have this bump under my left nipple". Donna said to me, "Ok, but you're always looking for something". Once she did agree to feel the area I was pointing to she responded with, "Ok, I feel it. It's probably a gland. I have them all the time. It's probably nothing".

I proceeded to explain that the area had been sore, etc. At that point she said, "well if you're worried about it, call Dr. Richardson's office and get it checked". She finished getting dressed and off to work she went. I had a later afternoon flight to New York's JFK airport, but I called my doctor's office to set up an appointment for Friday, upon my return from the Autism function.

The office had informed me at the time I called to make the appointment, that my doctor, Dr. Richardson, had left the practice. The only one who would be able to see me was the female Physician's Assistant. I agreed, with a little hesitancy. I am never really that comfortable with female doctors. I am not sure why, maybe it has to do with all those wonderful little prostate exams, guys my age need to have every year. I was in no position to let this stand in my way. I had to find out what was going on.

That Friday I arrived at the office and did the obligatory paperwork and weigh in. I sat in the exam room awaiting the door to open and the P.A. to come in. I had never met this woman before. Now, I had to explain to her what was troubling me.

I did.

She asked me to remove my shirt and lie flat on my back on the exam table. She placed her cold hand over the area I pointed out where I "thought" I felt this bump. She rotated her hands and fingers for what seemed to be about three seconds and said to me, "Well, I agree with your assessment that you have some type of lump there". These were not exactly the words I was hoping would come out of her mouth.

"Now What", I asked?

She said to me, "You need to get a mammogram".

This part caught me off guard. How the hell does a man get a mammogram? I've never had a mammogram and I don't know of any man who has had one or even witnessed one being given. I guess in my perverted mind (and maybe in other men's minds), I would have liked to witness one or two, but most of us had never seen it happening. My wife has certainly explained how "uncomfortable" it is to get hers done annually, but me?

She immediately had her receptionist call around to get it set up for me. She explained that although it could be nothing, she didn't want me to spend the weekend worrying about it. I wasn't 100% sure whether she was being totally honest with me. First of all I never met this woman until today. I didn't really know her or her medical style. I did sense that she was worried about this "lump".

The secretary set up all of the details and I immediately left the office and was off to the Imaging facility.

CHAPTER 2
CHILDHOOD AND DESTINY:

We all have experienced trepidation with medical tests and procedures. Besides being uncomfortable or painful in some cases, there's always the fear of what are they going to find? This experience was like no other for two main reasons.

First, I knew I had something there. I obviously didn't know exactly what this was but I did know it was something and something potentially serious. After all it was a lump. We all know that any lump could be a cancer. I have spent my whole life worrying about getting cancer. I have my reasons for this assumption and it goes way back into my childhood.

I am Jewish. In the Jewish faith, children are normally named after a close relative who has died. The newborn takes on the Hebrew name of that person or persons to which the parents wanted to honor. In my case, my mom wanted to honor her two brothers who both had died at an unreasonably young age. Herman and Isadore or "Izzy" were their names. Chiam and Israel were their Hebrew names.

I never really liked my name. After all, my friends all seemed to have normal cool names growing up. Mark, Matt, Michael, Jerry, or even my brother Jeff? How did they come up with Harvey? And then, tack on a middle name that I liked even less. Irwin! Who names a little kid Irwin? Why couldn't I have a basic name like everyone else? *Harvey* is for a six foot invisible rabbit or a cocktail, like a *Harvey Wallbanger*. People always joked and made fun of my name.

When I became old enough to raise the question to my parents as to why they named me Harvey Irwin, it irritated my mother immensely. After all, she was paying tribute to her dead brothers. It sincerely hurt her to have me not like my name. More importantly, it insulted her that I would actually question it. She continuously argued with me about it. Once she finally explained why and how her brothers had died, it left an indelible mark on my conscious. Neither my mom, nor anyone else in my life ever knew how I really felt about this fact.

No one!

Both of her brothers had died from cancer!

It's a secret I carried with me through my entire life. I had this innate fear that because I was named after two of my, would be uncles, who both passed on far too early and before I was born, I thought I was destined to have the same fate. I was destined to get cancer and die young.

This fear of dying young was pronounced and evident in my mind ever since I can remember. It really never went away, but for some reason once I passed forty, I felt like I had beaten the odds. Surely I must have, since neither Herman nor Izzy ever made it to forty years old.

There was so much more to my life as a child, many things that occurred and I suppressed, and did not realize until sessions with my Psychotherapist beginning in 2012.

What became exposed and evident to me was that my life as a child had so much trauma involve, both physical and mental and it was leaving permanent marks on my psychological being.

Being the middle child with an older brother and baby sister, I can tell you point blank that "middle child syndrome" does exist! Whether it was from the hand me down clothes or just not caring about me in general, I always felt that I was sort of neglected. As it turned out, for me it was a positive as it forced me in to becoming my own person. So I was the rebel of the family, and was treated as such. But it was really the opposite. I became a rebel to gain the attention that I felt I was not getting from my parents. Looking backwards I'm glad that I had to fen for myself. It taught me a lot about being on my own and becoming the man I am today.

At the ripe old age of four months, I had, what has been told to me was surgery to correct a "double hydro-seal", basically an infant hernia. This procedure was performed by a very famous doctor and man, one who would move on to become "Surgeon General of the USA, C. Everett Koop". I always thought that was pretty cool. The United States Surgeon General operated on me.

Following that I had some of the normal childhood stuff like my tonsils removed but I do recall being carted in and out of doctor's offices and hospitals for one procedure or another. I was a skinny kid and didn't really like to eat steak or any meat for that matter. I remember one time, I would take my cut up steak and kept tossing pieces under the kitchen table, thinking (or not thinking) that my parents would not find it there?

Duh!

I remember that my dad figured out what I was doing and made me eat all of the steak off the floor as a punishment. That certainly didn't enhance my taste for meat!

My parents always rented a summer place "down the shore" as we Philadelphian's call it. We would rent an apartment in Atlantic City, where the family could spend the summer days on the beach and nights on the boardwalk. My dad always told me how *lucky* we were to have this place "down the shore" and that my friends that got shipped off to camp or stayed home in hot Philadelphia should be jealous of us. Although I loved our summers there, I always felt like I missed out on playing little league. I always wanted to be a good baseball player. To this day, I feel like I could have been one and encouraged my own boys to play. My eldest son Matthew has proved my talents and instincts correct and had a great baseball career as a high school and as a collegiate player.

I made sure I was as involved as possible with my two boys in all of their athletic endeavors. I coached Matt starting from T-Ball at five years old and all the way up through American Legion baseball. I also coached him and Jameson in youth football (which I didn't know that much about since I never played youth football) as well as in basketball through their CYO and AAU years.

I was going to be there for my boys every step of the way and until I had to turn them over to the high school coaches. I know at the time my boys had some hesitancy as to why "dad" was always around and usually their coach. It must have seemed overwhelming to them to have me there so much, but I was going to give them everything I had. Every minute of my time because my dad never had any time to even sign me up or come to my games. I promised myself it would be different and it was.

I feel at this point in their lives that my two boys who may have had an issue with me always being their coach realize how positive it was for all of us! I know I not only influenced and helped them to succeed but it also had a positive effect on many of their friends as they grew older. I still often run into one of these kids who are now grown men and they'll stop me in the supermarket and say, "Hey, Coach Singer, how are you?" Some of them still post photos on Facebook of many of our championship winning teams. It brings a major smile to my face every time one recognizes me or posts an old photo. I know I had some influence on all of them, not only my own kids.

My dad would never let me sign up for little league because the season went into July and we would always leave right after school ended around the 3rd week of June. I remember one year defying his wishes and going to Tarken playground to sign myself up, forging my dad's signature. I just wanted to play so badly. I also remember the anger of my coach when I had to leave five weeks before the season ended! I was always the kid playing without his parents watching and caring, but at least I was playing.

Growing up in a row home in Philadelphia's northeast section had its benefits and its detractions. We had a great neighborhood in the Oxford Circle section of Philly. The streets were long and narrow and consisted of row homes about 35 on each side. When my parents and Aunt Lil and Uncle Joe purchased their houses they were new and cost about $7500.00.

Because it was a brand new neighborhood, most of the homes were filled with young children. It was literally a cement city with all of the homes being about 1500 square feet in total and all 35 on each side attached to one another. We all had these little lawns in the front along with about five steps up to the house. Most had a little patio in front of the living room window. The lawns took about five minutes to mow with those old "rotary" type push lawn mowers. There was very little room to "play" and there were all of these kids living just on our block.

We would invent games to play that didn't require a lot of space. We had games like "Wire-Ball". The entire length of the block had one single long wire that was about 20 feet up in the air. We would take a "Pinkie

Ball" (you may remember those pink rubber balls) or a "Pimple-Ball" (which was like a pinkie but was white and had little pimples on it) and one team member would throw the ball up in the air and attempt to hit the wire. If it hit the wire and no one caught it on the way down, it was a home run! If it didn't hit the wire you had to catch it in the air before it bounced to record an "out". If it bounced once it was a single, twice a double, etc. I can't imagine that throwing the ball straight up in the air could have been good for our shoulders but catching that little ball certainly helped to increase our eye-hand coordination. No baseball gloves were ever used.

We also had "Step-Ball". Where one team member would throw the Pinkie Ball against the three or five steps in front of the house and it would go into the street and you had to catch it before it hit ground. We also had "half-ball" where you cut the Pinkie or Pimple ball in half and we used old broom sticks as bats and had to hit the "half of a ball". This was much harder than you would think. I also recall that when you cut the Pimple ball in half, this yellow liquid would be inside. We were always warned that the liquid may be toxic or could cause cancer.

No, I don't believe that the cutting in half of those pimple balls caused my cancer.

At night in the summer we had a game called "Spring The Lever". Some people called it "Jail Break". I was never sure where the name came from but we would divide up into two teams and one group would head out while the others covered their eyes. After about two minutes the other team would have to go find the hiding team and bring them to "jail". Once in jail, we would have to rescue our teammates or "spring" them by sneaking up and attacking the jail and touching the hand of the detainee. Of course this game could go on for hours but always came to an abrupt halt when "Nate" the Jack 'n' Jill ice cream man rang his bell as he pulled onto Fanshawe Street.

Growing up in a row home in Northeast Philadelphia had its benefits, especially on Halloween. Do you know how many of the "real size candy bars" you can collect with 70 houses on one street and then multiply by the two streets on either side of ours? We would fill large pillowcases full of candy and then stop home and go back for another full case lot. Those Halloween paper bags they sold at the "5 and Dime store" wouldn't work because the load was much too heavy. I'm not sure how we all didn't become obese or diabetic from this one day a year's haul!

When we wanted a real basketball court and did not want to use the three phone lines that ran across all the homes in the back driveways as a basket, we hiked to Tarken or Max Myers playgrounds or to our elementary school, J. Hampton Moore. Our school also had "no grass", just a large cement area with some monkey bars and some baskets without any nets. At Tarken, we had nets but they were made of metal chains. I guess they lasted so much longer that way. "Ahh", I can still hear the sound of the ball going through the chain nets for a score.

Everything was so close. We were one block from Castor Avenue, with all the regular stores, gas stations and even our own movie theatre. Literally a three minute walk to all the conveniences one could ask for. The highlight of Castor Avenue was when Lenny's Hot Dogs opened on the corner of Fanshawe and Castor. They had the best hot dogs and you could smother them in "pepper-hash" or add a "fish-cake" to your order. To this day, I have never seen "pepper-hash" anywhere else or even mentioned?

You could take the 59B Bus, which was a bus that ran powered by the electric wires above (we could probably utilize these now seeing we're going back toward electric vehicles) and take the bus for 10 blocks up Castor Avenue to Cottman Avenue where you had a bowling alley and major department stores like Gimbels and Lit Brothers. I can't believe my parents let me do this, but I would go every Saturday morning on the 59B bus with my bowling ball bag in hand, all by myself at age 10 or 11 and bowl in the Saturday morning junior league. None of us would allow our 10 year olds today, to do this by themselves. It was such a different time in our lives.

Four Breast Cancer Survivors, My Mom, Aunt Ruth, Vicki and Me

CHAPTER 3
ATLANTIC CITY:

Atlantic City was our family's summer home. It was not like we had our own house "down the shore", but we went every summer and stayed in the Chelsea area of the city. We would usually stay on Boston Avenue in some apartment that my folks had rented for the entire summer. Some were a little bit cramped and others were more roomie. Whatever the place was for that summer we made it work.

My mom would spend most of the summer with us as she was a secretary in the Philadelphia School District and had summers off. My dad would usually come down on Friday night and immediately take us up to the boardwalk. Seymour (my dad) was the most proficient person ever when it came to winning toys and stuffed animals from the arcades and amusement parks like Million Dollar Pier.

This was the Atlantic City that existed long before gambling took over the town and way after the Boardwalk Empire days. Actually the 1950's and 60's were the apex of Atlantic City's existence. Clean boardwalk. Great stores, arcades and of course the Steel Pier diving horse all existed in those days.

Harvey, Jacque and Brother Jeff- 1968 –Boston Ave in Atlantic City,

Seymour would arrive around 5:00 PM on Friday evening as we were just getting off the beach. A quick shower for all of us and we couldn't wait to go with dad and "walk the boards" and anticipate coming home with a giant bear or other stuffed creature. Somehow when those large wheels with 160 numbers on them spun, Seymour figured out how to actually push the buttons in front that eventually caused the wheel to stop. It was amazing! 160 numbers and he would basically put a nickel on a group of numbers that were together on the wheel and cover 10 or so numbers. 50 Cents a Spin! He would practice first hitting the little button and using his keen vision to see where the numbers crossed a certain point on the wheel and how long it would take to slow down and eventually stop. Once he had the "formula" he would begin investing his .50 cents per spin. Usually, within 5.00 or 7.00 dollars he would hit a winner! You could see the four of us walking back toward Chelsea carrying two or three of these giant pandas, six foot long snakes or a tiger, on any given Friday evening.

Mom stayed behind most Friday nights as this was her downtime since she had the kids all week. Well she didn't really have to watch us on her own as my parents would actually employ some teenage girl to also spend the summer with us and act as nanny. After all, my mom couldn't possibly watch the three of us all over the beach, while sunbathing and playing cards with her friends. This also allowed my parents to go out on the town to places like Club Harlem, the 500 Club or just hang in the parked rolling chairs eating sunflower seeds all evening as they watched the people go by.

As I got older of course I wanted more independence to go up on the boardwalk by myself. This also caused a need for more than the $1.00 or $2.00 dollar allowance my dad would give me. So at the ripe old age of 13, my parents suggested I get a job. This seemed like it was a little early and hell, it was my vacation too, but I really wanted the money.

My first job in Atlantic City was working in a laundromat! Yes, one of those commercial places with about 50 washers and dryers that were coin operated. A friend of my parent's friends hooked me up. In those days they didn't have automated coin changers or even the machines that sold the little boxes of soap. Very few people who spent their summer in Atlantic

City had a washer and especially not a dryer. They all used the laundromat and spent one day a week on this chore for their family. So my first job was to sit in the back room on this half-round beaten up, old couch and wait for someone to ring the bell for change or to purchase the small box of "All" detergent. I did this for three days a week and mostly during the day when all of my friends were having fun on the beach. I really hated it! It was totally boring as I sat there reading comic books, usually Archie, which was my favorite. What ever happened to Jughead, anyway? He must have run off with the hot blonde Betty. I never did like the "boys" comic books with all of those super-hero's in them. Maybe that was my feminine side coming out?

What I did enjoy was that at the end of each week, I had some $10 or $15 dollars in my pocket to blow on the boardwalk.

Eddie, who was the owner of the Kelvinator Laundromat, taught me how to fix the common things that may go wrong with the washers and even how to start them without using the quarter and dime that it was set for. Eddie also taught me a few life lessons that my dad didn't have the time to share with me or didn't have any interest in sharing. Eddie was about 15 years younger than my dad and had two baby girls at home. I was like the "son" with whom he could play and teach some female life lessons. I listened intently as I never had any other adult male explain so much about life and girls to me.

Eddie's laundromat began to evolve as he figured out that "his big washers" up front, could be used to wash towels for some of the smaller motels on the island. Atlantic City is not an island by itself but is actually "on an island" that is comprised of four cities. In addition to Atlantic City there is Ventnor, Margate and Longport. Today, the further away from Atlantic City you get the more expensive the real estate becomes on the island.

In those days there were a few big hotels like the President, the Deauville and the Chalfont-Haddon Hall, but mostly the streets were filled with 30-50 room motels.

As Eddie's commercial business grew with more and more motels becoming customers, his laundromat business became less important. I worked for Eddie from the age of 13 for pretty much every summer including through college. He eventually sold the laundromat business and moved to a facility in a "not so nice" area of Atlantic City and bought a former diaper service laundry. The diaper service had much larger machines and this enabled us to wash more towels or sheets at one time. We actually did wash diapers for one year until Eddie realized there was much more money doing business with the hotels and motels full time. I became a full time summer employee. Eddie would pick me up at 7:30 AM and drop me off after our last few stops around 5:00 PM. Basically I only had Sunday and one other week day off to enjoy the beach, which always bothered me. What didn't bother me was I was now earning $120.00 or $150.00 per week and had plenty of cash to spend on the boardwalk usually gambling it away on Skee Ball.

I became a Skee Ball professional and I would hang out in Hi-Hat Joe's arcade waiting on unsuspecting patsies to play me for a dime or a quarter in a Skee-Ball contest. I could roll a 450 (a perfect score) seven out of 10 times. It usually didn't take 450 to beat my opponent, usually 360 points was enough. (nine balls hitting the 40 point box each) This was Seymour, my dad's blood, running through me.

The one summer I couldn't work for Eddie was the year I had a double-hernia surgery. Working for Atlantic Laundry was a physically taxing job. Our washers didn't have a spin-cycle. You basically had to empty these 250 pound capacity washers with totally saturated towels and sheets and hand carry them to an extractor. An extractor was a big spinning machine to wring the water out and before moving them to the dryers. That summer I needed to work but had to be careful to not have a job that was physically demanding.

My dad was also a "bingo" expert. In those days, there were about four different bingo joints on the boardwalk. They showed these prizes you could win by playing bingo on the boardwalk, but they really never paid with "prizes". They paid with "CASH"! Yes, illegally. It was gambling long before legalized Atlantic City gambling. My dad would spend all night on certain Friday and Saturday evenings in the Golden Nugget playing 20 bingo cards at a time. This was his preferred place of chance. He knew everyone in the place so when I needed a non-physical job, he was able to hook me up as a ball-boy or collector in one of their sister bingo joints.

I was working the evening shift which was different for me after all of those years of working days. I was 19 at this point. Early on in July, our "caller", the guy who sits up in the pedestal chair and calls out the number over the microphone, took ill. The manager approached me and said, "I like your deep voice, do you think you could fill in as the number caller"? I gave it a try and they loved me and I loved doing it. I felt so large sitting up on that pedestal and saying "*Num--ber-- 12--- First Row*".

They soon found a more "mature" replacement and asked me if I wanted to move to days? I guess I just wasn't old enough to present the image they wanted with their night patrons, who were much more experienced and when the bingo room was much busier.

My job evolved from just "calling the numbers" to attempting to "BARK" people into our place off the boardwalk in the height of the summer days. People didn't really want to sit inside on a beautiful summer day especially when the beach and ocean were steps away. They had a separate speaker protruding out onto the boardwalk and I would have to attempt to get some people into our place to play "bingo".

"COME ON IN OFF THAT HOT BOARDWALK...IT'S COOL AND COMFORTABLE HERE ON THE INSIDE... IT'S OLD FASHION FIVE IN A LINE BINGO ALL AFTERNOON AND EVENING LONG, IN AIR-CONDITIONED COMFORT. YES... YOU TOO... COULD BE OUR NEXT BIG WINNER!"

I must have repeated those lines a hundred times or more per day, five days per week. Those words are indelible in my brain.

While in college between my freshman and sophomore year I decided I was going to live with a few friends and escape my parent's apartment and their control. Hell, I had plenty of money to support myself and pay my quarter of the apartment. Howard, Marty and a guy I didn't know all that well named Gary, found a great ground floor apartment on South Montpelier Avenue, one block from the beach. The apartment had two large bedrooms and each had two double beds. We only had one bathroom, but a big living room and a decent little kitchen. There were steps that went up to the rest of the four story house where the other apartments were housed. The beach house was owned by a Rabbi and his wife and renting to some nice Jewish boys from Philadelphia made sense to them. The Rabbi and his wife also had one child, a daughter. Let's just say that the daughter who sported red curly hair and kind of weird body wasn't the most attractive girl on the street. We used to joke about who had the guts to "do the Rabbi's daughter"? As the summer progressed the Rabbi's daughter became a running joke for all of us. We knew that one of us would take the plunge at some point that summer.

One Sunday afternoon while we all were having a great day on the beach, Howard said to us that he was going to head back to the apartment and catch some of the Phillies game on TV. We all thought that it was a little strange to leave the beach on such a perfect "beach day" but this is what he wanted to do, and Howard always marched to his own beat. About an hour later I decided to head back and catch the last couple of innings as the game was close and hangout with Howard.

CHELSEA BEACH (1969)

When I entered the apartment the TV in the living room was not on and there was no sign of Howie. I started watching the game, grabbed a cold one and settled in. Suddenly, I heard some noise coming from behind the other bedroom door, Howard and Gary's room. Guess who was in there with the Rabbi's daughter?

All I remember are the words, **"But Harv, she was so grateful!"**

The steps that headed up to the rest of the beach-house became our display for all of the wine and liquor bottles we consumed. We did our share of partying in those days but nothing out of the ordinary for the times. Some pot. Some Quaaludes. Some hash. You know the normal stuff to party with in the summer of 1973.

I was home alone on the night of August 1st as my other three room-mates worked as waiters for the restaurants and hotels down the shore and mostly worked nights when the tips were better. I was still working for Eddie's Atlantic Laundry during the daytime. I hear this knock on my door and I go to answer it and there's this strange looking guy who must have been 40 or so years old. I go to the door and he says to me, "Is Gary here?"

Gary was the roommate I knew very little about. I responded, "no, I think Gary went home to Philly for the night". "Shit", he says, "cause I wanted buy some stuff". At this point he just turned and walked away. I quickly stuck my head out and then went out and sort of followed him as he disappeared around the corner. Something wasn't right! Although I didn't know Gary all that well, I did know or thought I did, that he wasn't the kind of guy to be dealing drugs. He partook like the rest of us but no one was selling. There was a very large dividing line in those days and you don't want to be caught selling, especially not in Atlantic City with one of the most ruthless police departments around.

Gary was in Philadelphia that evening but when my other roommates came home I told them about the "guy that wanted to buy some stuff". It didn't add up and we decided that this guy was probably a "Narc". (short for narcotics agent). We quickly decided that this wasn't the time to take any chances and we cleaned the apartment of what we thought was all the illegal pot and paraphernalia. I had the keys to Eddie's laundry so we took everything down to the laundry and stashed it there.

The next day was my birthday, August 2nd. We kept our partying to "legal things" and went out to the Melody Lounge, our favorite hangout which was a dance club with a live band. No signs of the Narc or anything else suspicious that day and all seemed well.

It wasn't!

The following evening around 7:30 or so, my older brother Jeff, and some others were over visiting and hanging out, listening to cranked up Led Zeppelin when I decided to take a shower and get ready for the rest of the nights festivities. I was in the shower and I heard my brother Jeff yell, *"Harv, we have company... You need to get out here now"*. "Now", I thought? But I'm in the middle of my shower? I heard him say "now" again and before I knew it, the shower curtain was ripped back and I was naked, staring at a guy with a GUN POINTED AT ME and with a German Shepherd at his side. "FREEZE" he says to me. "Put Your Hands Above Your Head".

"Freeze", like where am I going, naked, with a gun and a dog pointing at me? I quickly realized that my "Narc" instincts were correct.

So they handcuff me, after first allowing me to put on some clothes, and they started badgering me about "where the shit is hiding". Now I know that we cleaned out and there wasn't any "shit" that they were looking for in the apartment. They didn't care. They proceeded to dump out every drawer in every room. They tipped over the fridge and threw all the contents all over the kitchen. They went up the stairs where we had all of our bottles and crashed them all as they went. After about an hour all they came up with was one hash pipe that Gary had hiding in the bottom of his underwear drawer, and we missed while we cleaned out. They also found "one Quaalude" that was in an upside down Disney World hat on the dresser in the other bedroom. Surely, they weren't going to book me for anything like that?

Wrong again!

Once they had that warrant and trashed the place they had to book us on something. They knew where both of my roommates were working and immediately picked them up right in front of their employers and patrons and the three of us went off to Atlantic City jail. I guess they had been staking us out for days. Ironically, Gary was the only guy not picked up, because he wasn't at work and still back in Philly that night.

Now I had never been in jail before (nor since for that matter) and it wasn't a fun experience. I didn't call my dad because I figured he would beat the crap out of me. So my one call went to Eddie! Eddie came down and bailed us out, but not before spending some five hours locked up.

The highlight of jail was when we asked if the three of us could at least share a cell while we were waiting to get bailed out. "No" was the response from the turnkey who assigned the cells. "Only two to a cell", we were told. So there we were three scared 19 year olds and one of us had to go it alone. How would we decide?

So while standing there about ready to be processed and assigned a cell, we decided to play the game of "1-2-3 Shoot". This was a way of choosing sides and teams while growing up in Philly. You count to three and then each of us throws out one or two fingers and the one that doesn't match the other two loses. YEP... I lost! I ended up in a cell with some wino they found sleeping on a park bench somewhere in Atlantic City. So not only was I in a jail cell, I was in there with some smelly old guy who reeked from booze.

The case was basically ridiculous. They had nothing on me since the one pipe and the one "Quaalude", were found in the other bedroom. I still had to pay an attorney and eventually we were able to get the case thrown out and the records expunged. I was never found guilty of anything.

Additionally what also was thrown out, were the four of us! We were of course evicted from the apartment and the landlord confiscated the rest of the season's rent money to pay for the damage to the apartment done by Atlantic City's finest. I ended up living with Eddie for the remainder of the summer at his home off shore. I guess he couldn't afford to lose me in the middle of summer. Marty went back to living with his family at their apartment down the shore and Howard went back to Philly and then on to New York City to live and work with his cousin for the remainder of the summer.

To this day we're not 100% sure why they targeted us or Gary specifically, but we think it was because some guy, who Gary used to "buy" some pot from, was busted about a week or so before us. We think he was trying to cover his own ass and tried to lessen his punishment by telling the Narcotics Unit that Gary was "his supplier". Gary wasn't his supplier and a year later he joined the Navy and I have no idea what became of him since.

Chapter 4
ONE HEALTH ISSUE AFTER ANOTHER:

I recall how my brother and sister would spend all summer down the shore and I would have to go back to Philadelphia to see doctors while they played on the beach.

My health issues were certainly built from my childhood onward. This added to my innate fear of getting Cancer and dying young. After spending most of my childhood seeing one doctor or another, I still managed to keep moving forward with my life.

During my freshman year of college, I had a double-hernia operation. (I'm not sure if this was a product of my childhood Hydro-seal or not) It wasn't a "usual" operation for a 19 year old college kid, but I got through the surgery which always seemed fairly normal to me. I did do something pretty stupid after that surgery, recovering at home my girlfriend came over to keep me company and I convinced her to engage in some sexual activity. This turned out to be a hell of a lot more painful than pleasurable! Heck I was young and any opportunity for sex I was going for. I never remembered the doctors or nurses telling me I needed to refrain from having sex, post hernia surgery. I guess either they assumed I couldn't be that stupid or that I was just not sexually active.

I spent a lot of time being sick as a kid. I never really remembered what I had or what it was all about, but I know that I saw what seemed to be ten times as many doctors as my brother and sister. My biggest issue of memory was this Pilonidal Cyst. I had it drained a couple of times when "Cousin Craig" the doctor referred me to some surgeon friend of his that was still in the process of perfecting a new surgery for these cysts. Basically instead of "draining" it and allowing it to heal over a two week period, he would actually cut open the area and remove the entire cyst. It all seemed quite intriguing except for one problem, the incision never completely closed, mostly due to where it was located at the base of my spine. I think I had an open wound there for about five years! To this day, they still treat Pilonidal Cysts by opening it and draining it naturally over the next few weeks. I guess Dr. Craig's buddy's surgery never caught on.

Additionally, about seven years later I had a full laminectomy of my L-5/S-1 disks, basically full back surgery. I was living in California at the time and I remember sneezing and having this pain go down my leg. I didn't think too much of it at the time as the pain subsided, but about a year later my entire body was crooked, trying to alleviate itself from the "blown disk" pain. After four months of attempting to avoid surgery utilizing acupuncture and physical therapy, I gave in and had the laminectomy. It took almost six months to recover and to this day I still incur some off and on back pain issues. My scar is about seven inches long down my back. Today's surgery for the same condition leaves you with a one or one and a half inch scar and usually only about six weeks of real rehab.

For all the trauma I had been through health wise, I always found it strange that I never broke a bone or had to wear a cast? I'm guessing probably because I had so little time playing organized sports or maybe I was just "lucky" in that respect. I guess I had enough "other stuff" to make up for it.

Chapter 5
GO WEST YOUNG MAN

After college I decided I had to leave home and Philadelphia. I had attended Temple University for four and a half years and lived at home at my parent's house for the entire time. I had pretty much the freedom to do what I wanted and to come and go as I pleased without too much explanation.

It was the height of the disco and drug culture years and I can honestly say my friends and I made the most of it. We had our planned places to party and dance.

On Thursday nights we went to *The Classroom*, an aptly named discothèque in an office building environment). My group of buds would travel not far from our homes in Northeast Philadelphia together. We would stop and drink, actually guzzle, whole bottles of Yago San Gria on some side street. This saved us the costs of getting a buzz at the bar there. Money was certainly at a premium for us. Once Murray puked on some poor lady's front lawn, we knew we were ready to go!

Friday nights we went to the "*Library*", a very cool club on City Line Ave, the high class area of Philadelphia. I guess we needed some place to "study" what we had learned at the "*Classroom*" the night before! The "Library" was always so crowded and packed in with people, that dancing was basically an exercise of standing in place and attempting to move to the beat.

Saturday Nights were my favorite. We went to "*Artemis*", a tight two-story club on Sansom Street in downtown Philadelphia. **Artemis** was better than all the other clubs because the crowd was totally different. We didn't know everyone in the place and that made it easier to pick up on some strange girls. We even had a Sunday place called *Dimples*, which was in the Northeast and only three blocks from my parent's house. We didn't always frequent *Dimples* or anyplace on Sunday because our bodies were often spent from the Thursday, Friday and Saturday partying. Some nights I came home, some nights I crashed at some girl's place I picked up, or at a buddy's house.

It took me four and half years to finish college because I had always been directed by my parents, that I, like most Jewish boys of the 60's, were supposed to be doctors. My cousin Craig was a doctor and look how successful he was? One and half years and after my second semester of organic chemistry I realized that I had NO CLUE WHAT I WAS DOING. Hell, I didn't even know how I had passed the first two semesters? It was time to reevaluate my academic priorities.

I spent the next semester taking classes from all different departments at Temple University. I took such great educational classes as "Male Liberation-Images Through Film". This was a study of old James Cagney type movies. We basically watched old male dominated films and discussed them. No Tests. No Papers. No studying. NO PROBLEM!

It was during this "trial balloon" semester that I took my first writing course. Journalism 101.

"WOW, this is a piece of cake" I thought and I actually liked going to class enjoying what we were doing. Writing came easily to me. The assignments were handed out and in about 45 minutes, I could bang out a story. My GPA went from barely above 2.0 to 3.0 and near 3.5. I breezed through the final two and a half years of college. So what if I graduated six months after most of my friends. It was no big deal and because I was working all the way through my last three years of college I always had cash for gas or for drinks at the "**Library**" or to buy some pot.

But once I did finally graduate (it was December 1976) I spent the next three months working in all kinds of shady but lucrative jobs. One was selling advertising on behalf of the "Police and Fireman's Association" in a magazine or booklet that was actually never published. It was like taking candy from a baby selling this stuff by calling unsuspecting businesses and telling them that I'm "Officer O'Reilly" and "can you help out the boys"? In return, we'll give you some fake FOP (Fraternal Order of Police) sticker to put on your car and next time you get stopped, show the sticker and it will get you out of a ticket! Yea, Right! I didn't care. I was raking in some good cash and despite all of my partying vices, I was able to pull together about $2000.00

"Ahhh", $2000.00, the magic number that was going to get me the hell out of Philadelphia and be able to head to California. I had always wanted to go and see California and the thoughts of beach and women were always calling me. Spending all of my college years living at home added to my drive to go somewhere else to live, somewhere new and exciting.

I continuously asked all of my closer friends if they would leave Philly with me and move to California. No one wanted to take the chance. Some had full time, post college jobs. Some just didn't have the balls. Some thought I was totally crazy, but I had to do it.

Finally I got, not a close friend, but Howard's cousin named Andy, her ex-husband, Ronny, who said he would drive his beat up old 1961 BMW 2002 and I would drive my recently purchased 1965 Type 3 Fastback VW with its Earl Sheib, canary yellow, $ 99.00 paint job, across the country separate, but together. Of course we were communicating by those cool CB Radio's. **"Breaker-Breaker One-Nine Good Buddy".** We would split some sleazy motel rooms along the route.

Andy was a very close cousin of Howard and Marty, two of my closest friends. Ronny and Andy were always together it seemed, but once they were married for some reason it all seemed to fall apart.

I wanted to mention Andy here because Andy recently passed away after fighting Ovarian Cancer for many years. She was a sweetheart of a woman and Ronny really didn't deserve her. Her passing hit very hard with Howard and Marty. Ovarian cancer is a very deadly disease as it doesn't usually present symptoms until the disease has spread. Just another cancer patient fallen to the medical community but an extremely huge loss to her family and friends. RIP Andy!

As luck would have it, two days before we were to leave, my VW had issues. Expensive issues! It needed a valve-job. Of course I had no idea what a valve-job was but I did know it was about to cost me about half of my total savings. My $2000.00 savings account was down to about $950.00. But much to my mom's dismay, I was going anyway. She really didn't try that hard to talk me out of it, figuring that I would run out of money within the first few weeks and be headed back home. As for my dad, I'm not even sure he knew I left. That's how disconnected my relationship was with my father. I know he loved me, but he never really showed it. We weren't a very huggy, warm type of family. I think this affected me and how I reacted to growing up in their household.

Ronny and I left on a Friday. We took the southern route across the country that was mapped out by my folk's AAA Club trip-ticket. By day two my butt was so sore that I didn't know how I was going to make it the rest of the way. It wasn't your normal "sore-butt" but it was a re- inflammation from my Pilonidal Cyst that was just another of my childhood surgeries. It bothered me on and off most of my teenage years but the 12-14 hour daily driving had totally aggravated it. I don't think those VW Seats offered too much comfort or support to assist either.

We arrived in Los Angeles on Wednesday evening and checked into some cheap motel in Hollywood. The first thing I did was look in the phone book to find some surgeon that would drain this cyst! I had the cyst drained several times over the past 10 years and I knew what I needed to have done. I ended up seeing some "butcher of a doctor" in Santa Monica the next day. After a 20 minute lecture by this doctor and how I shouldn't be moving to L.A. and why "us easterner's should just stay the hell away and head back home", he pulled out a scalpel and without the aid of any anesthetics proceeded to cut a huge "X" into my backside cyst. Talk about painful! I believe to this day he purposely did not use anything to numb me and just wanted to invoke as much pain as possible in order to get me to leave L.A.

It didn't work.

That following Sunday morning, I rushed out to buy the L.A. Times and scoured through the help wanted ads looking for a job. I knew I had about two to three weeks of cash to survive. If I didn't find someone to pay me to do something I was going to have to call my parents and beg them to send me money to get back home to Philadelphia. Plus I couldn't bear to think about making that drive again.

I spotted an ad for a salesman for a Publisher's Representative Company. Of course I had no idea what a "Publisher's Rep" company was. Ok I knew I could sell as I worked for most of my college life as a salesman at The Gent Limited, a men's haberdashery inside a large mall in Oxford Valley, PA. I learned a lot about selling and about clothing working there and to this day I am still quite proficient at matching up shirts and ties to go with nice suits.

I called the number on Monday morning and a very nice female voice provided me with basic information that the job was to sell advertising space for publications, mostly magazines that they represented.

Bang, magazines!

I had a journalism degree and I sold fake ads for the Police and Fire Association. This sounded like a match to me!

She gave me a time for my appointment and their address: 8852 Sunset Boulevard- fourth floor.

I put on my best clothes (the only dress clothes I had with me) and somehow found my way to 8852 Sunset Blvd. There was no GPS in those days. It was a six story building with the words "CROCKER BANK" on top. It was literally right on Sunset Strip across the street from Tower Records and down the block from Dick Clark Productions. Dick Clark, a Philadelphia institution had moved out to L.A. and I guess I was just following in his footsteps.

I didn't have the time to get nervous but when I got off the elevator on the fourth floor the nerves hit me. On the wall facing me as I exited the elevator were two sets of lettering. One said: <u>J.P. Publishers Representative Company.</u> The other sign said: <u>PENTHOUSE MAGAZINE</u>. Wow, was I really interviewing for Penthouse Magazine?

I didn't have a resume'. I'm not even sure I knew what a resume' was in those days. I filled out the three pages of application the receptionist gave me and I sat there for probably an hour in the outer lobby before finally being called into the offices.

They escorted me back, much to my dismay not to the Penthouse side of the floor, and I was greeted by this large man sitting behind the biggest flat-top desk I had ever seen. Something out of a movie set. I slumped into this large but very soft chair in front of him while he perused my application. This guy had on an open collared dress shirt, gold bracelets and a gold watch. He also had these giant gold chains around his neck. The largest of the chains had this lion's head which probably weighed about half a pound all by itself. I nervously gazed around this massive office. There was a large fish tank with piranha fish in it. There was a huge picture window with a view looking south toward Santa Monica Blvd. And there were pictures and statues of lions everywhere.

The man finally looked up. He stares me directly in the eyes and says; "What's your sign"?

What?

"Sign, what kind of sign", I remember thinking.

Then it hit me.

He wanted to know my astrological sign. It was the1970's you know. I looked around the room and once again saw all of the lions and a smile came over me. "I'm a Leo" I quickly and firmly stated. "Great, I like that" he replied. A few more seconds elapsed and he then asked me, "What does your father do for a living"? Smile again, "he's a salesman" I said. "I like that too", he responded. A couple more insignificant questions later and he said to me, "I think you'll work, you start tomorrow!"

I never even heard or even cared about the salary. I should have cared because it was only $600.00 per month, but all that mattered was that I had a job, in L.A., on Sunset Boulevard and I was starting tomorrow!

As things turned out, Jeff was a trailblazer. Jeff was a Chicago kid that moved to Los Angeles and became the one and only salesman for Penthouse

Magazine when Penthouse was nothing but a speck on the wall attempting to steal some of the market share of readers and advertisers from Playboy.

Bob Guccione had started up this skin magazine to compete somehow with Hugh Hefner's mega-enterprise. Jeff was taxed to find advertisers for this start- up venture and this was going to be no easy task.

After about nine months, Penthouse figured out that they needed an angle. They needed some way of drawing readers that Playboy did not have. Something new and exciting!

Let the "Great Pubic Hair War" begin!

Penthouse quickly realized that they had no chance going head to head with Playboy and surviving. Yes, both publications showed beautiful woman with their breasts exposed, but Playboy was a complete enterprise. They had clubs and a world recognizable bunny symbol that Penthouse had no chance of competing with. How were they to gain a piece of this business? Then it happened. Penthouse decided to go full frontal nudity. Disgusting to many I'm sure back in the late 60's, but guys bought it!

Boy did they buy it, to the tune of millions of copies per month. Jeff had this neatly authored contract where he received 15% commission on every ad that ran in the monthly magazine. He was their one and only salesman and his contract still had a number of years left to follow.

Advertisers flocked to Penthouse to reach all of those millions of deprived men who lived vicariously through their pages. The magazine went from publishing editions with about 36 pages to editions with 144+ pages. Most of those pages were advertising! Jeff got rich! Very, very rich!

Playboy had to respond as they were losing market share and fast. At first, they tried to protect the Playboy name and came out with a Skin Pub- lication called OUI' Magazine. "OUI'" didn't produce anywhere near the sales numbers they had hoped for so they also began showing full frontal nudity in their pictorials within Playboy. This was of course followed up with a new start up publication, by a guy named Larry Flynt, and what he coined as "HUSTLER" magazine. Hustler took it another step further and actually did close ups and what we would call today, airbrushing. And of course, along came "Playgirl", for the females and the gay guys.

The "Great Pubic Hair Wars" were in full force. Once PENTHOUSE began to grip and they had to pay Jeff, what in their opinion was "far too much money" every month, they offered him an exit package and made him an independent representative. Basically he would work on a commission basis only as a subcontractor. He would only be paid for those advertisers that were based in the eleven western states. Additionally, he could bring on and work for other magazines to build and support his independent business.

Ironically when Jeff employed me, he no longer had anything to do with Penthouse. But he used Penthouse to springboard his independent Publisher Representative business. Most of the magazines in those days were based in New York City or on the East coast. None of these magazines wanted to set up another office in L.A. or employ and pay their own advertising sales staff to be based there. The west coast market was growing but it wouldn't justify a separate office. So they hired an independent contractor to be their sales office for the west coast. J.P. Publishers Rep Company.

When I was hired, J.P. had about 150 Magazines that they sold the space for in the eleven western states. "Sold" was a term I will use loosely as Jeff didn't as much "Sell" as he did "Collect". He would spend most of his day just going through every edition of the magazines he represented and any ad that had a west coast address in its tagline, he would invoice back to the publisher. What a racket he had going. Jeff hired me and others like me and assigned us such mainstream titles as: "Working Craftsman". "American Kennel Gazette". "Broward County Life", a City Magazine for Southern Florida. We would generate "call reports" that were basically triplicate forms and send one copy back to the publisher. This made it look like they actually had salespeople working on their magazines. Each one of us had about 20 magazines that we worked for, even though every magazine thought that we were working for only theirs and possibly one or two others.

It didn't matter. I had a job and I wasn't moving back to Philadelphia anytime soon. I was going to prove to my parents and all of my doubters that I could do this. I could survive in Los Angeles on my own!

Jeff and Penthouse were still friends. Although to this day, I'm not sure how? The 4th floor of the Crocker Bank Building was 75% J.P. offices and 25% the west coast editorial office for Penthouse.

This 22 year old kid from Philadelphia would spend his lunch hour with Toni Guccione (Bob's Daughter) reading through the bags of Forum letters that would arrive daily. Yes, they actually do get hundreds of letters every day with all sorts of sexually deviant behavior stories. It was not unusual to pop out of the elevator only to find them doing a naked photo shoot in the other elevator or in the hallway.

Jeff was an eccentric guy and a total hypochondriac. He always thought he was going to get some bad disease because he had it so good. He had the house in Hollywood Hills with his wife. He had another house in Malibu with some girlfriend. He had a 280 SL convertible Mercedes and a Rolls Royce. Jeff used to give me the keys to his Rolls Royce and tell me to go down to his bank on Wilshire Blvd and drop the deposit of checks from those east coast publishers. I happily took those assignments.

One day I pulled up next to this convertible Mercedes in Jeff's Rolls, and Jacqueline Smith (of Charlie's Angels Fame) was driving it. We exchanged smiles. I'm guessing I was smiling more than she.

Every Friday afternoon Caesars would send the private jet to fetch Jeff and bring him to Vegas. He was a whale with a bankroll and he loved to throw the dice!

One year I went with him to Las Vegas for the CES (Computer Electronic Show). This was the place where all the "high-tech" people and companies assembled to display and sell their wares.

J.P. Publisher's Representative Company sold ads for Radio-Electronics magazine, a pop culture monthly for the hand radio and burgeoning early on computer industry. Mostly the advertisers sold parts, all kinds of electronic parts. Many of these companies were based in the Los Angeles or the San Francisco Bay area. They would purchase two, three or four pages of nothing but mail-order circuits and other electronic parts I knew nothing about.

The convention was always quite the experience of "high-tech-ness". I remember one night Jeff and I were meeting for dinner. We stopped in the hotel casino for a "little action" prior to dinner. I liked to gamble and was taught many gambling lessons from my dad who was a pretty sharp player himself. His biggest problem was that he never had the cash to back up his passion. Jeff did.

So Jeff and I were at the crap table. He had a pretty good bank-roll going on to the positive. It came his turn to throw the dice. He looked at me and said, "you throw them for me". I had no money in play so I wouldn't normally be entitled to throw the dice. I began a decent roll, a couple of come out 7's and 11's for instant money. And then a couple of passes to where Jeff was pressing his bets up and up. He must have had seven or eight grand in play. I threw the dice and BOOM a "SEVEN". All his money was gone.

He turned sternly toward me and said. "That's it, YOU'RE FIRED! You just cost me eight big".

I think he was serious for about 20 minutes, which I couldn't believe. But then he recounted and "re-hired" me. Talk about Psycho-Boss!

Apple Computers were just being invented. The publisher from Radio Electronics really wanted the Apple account as an advertiser. I remember flying up to Cupertino, CA to pitch the Apple account to advertise in Radio Electronics. The preparation and meeting went well except for the fact that Apple believed that computers weren't only going to be just for the electronic enthusiasts but they were also going to be more main stream. This was 1978. We left the meeting and laughed at these guys because they believed that our readers who were electronics buffs weren't going to be enough. They were going to buy ads in Playboy and reach all men. "What a stupid ad philosophy I remember thinking" as we headed back to L.A. "These guys are idiots!"

Ok, so I was a little bit WRONG as we all know today. Apple and Steve Jobs seemed to have succeeded despite my doubt and Radio Electronics magazine.

I spent the first year in California getting acclimated and trying to survive on that measly $600.00 per month. I didn't have any real friends and Ronny, the guy I traveled west with lasted about two weeks in that month to month apartment we rented in West Hollywood. One day I came home from work and he and all of his belongings were gone. All that he left me was a note that read, "I can't deal with it! Heading to Colorado, good Luck". Well at least he prepaid his part of our first month's rent

No great loss to me.

Michael Richardson, who was a New Yorker that moved out to L.A. about a year before me, shared the office next to mine. They were actually little offices, unlike today's cubicles. Michael left his family's sundry business in New York City for the glitz, glamour and weather of Southern California.

Michael and I became good friends even though his attorney roommate was a total ass. Mike convinced me after a month in this not so nice place in West Hollywood, among the hookers and the up and coming gay community, that my money would go much further if I moved to the Valley. The San Fernando Valley is the area just north of Los Angeles and where many of the working stiffs of L.A. reside and commute over Benedict or Coldwater Canyon into the city each day.

He was living in Van Nuys and I spent one Saturday going around Van Nuys to search out a furnished apartment, one preferably with a little bit of social life for 20 something's and with a pool. I found a nice neat SINGLE or STUDIO apartment. Single apartments or more like efficiencies. You have a small kitchen, a sofa that converts to a bed in a living room type setting, and a decent bathroom. What more did I need, especially on my $600 per month salary.

The apartment itself was adequate, but the social life around the apartment became the best part. Most of the people were single and living alone. We would meet up on weekends by the pool and became a friendly group. We would spend weekends together and even take ski trips together to Big Bear and Mammoth Mountain. Of course I had never skied before, but my new friends taught me the basics. Everyone was very friendly and fairly lonely. Sex became a product of "Friends with Benefits". We would all go out on the weekend and the ones that came back alone would knock on someone's door for a night-cap quickie. Hey, we were all friends, just helping one another out.

One guy living in the apartment complex was a recently divorced guy named Rich. Rich and I became very good friends even though we really had nothing in common. He was a banker, working for Carte Blanche and Citi-Corp. He couldn't cook. He had no social life since being divorced and was really a low key guy.

Rich reveled in my life style of hitting the disco's on the weekend nights. I started bringing him along with me to my special club in the valley called Tiffany's.

Tiffany's had the reputation of a "party club" with "loose women". I, being from the Philadelphia disco club circuit found these women "easy prey". Sometimes I would be so forward as to have a couple of dances and then head out to the parking lot for a quickie and back into the club for more action. Some nights I was just so loose and ready I would introduce myself and say, "Hi, I'm Harvey… Wanna Fuck?" It actually worked one night when the response was, "No, but I'll give you head in your car".

On most nights it was fairly easy to find "companionship". On the nights when that didn't happen, I could go back to our apartment complex and knock on Rita's door and she would pretty much accept me in for a late night-cap.

Tiffany's also had been known for throwing a wild party in Palm Springs every July 4th weekend.

No one of sane mind would want to vacation in Palm Springs in July because it was 110-120 degrees on average, every day. They had all of these rooms to fill and Tiffany's accommodated them by renting out the entire Palm Springs Rivera Hilton Hotel for the three day weekend. I had never attended, but the reputation was that it was quite the wild party.

By this time, Donna (who would later become my wife) and I had started dating. Donna moved into the building a few months after I did and became a part of the "group". We were friends who became good friends, but that's all it was. I would constantly tease Donna and ask "Do you want to spend the night". It was all a joke until one night she responded, "Yes, Ok". The friendship part was gone. We were dating, although it was occasionally at that point.

Martha, who was the manager of the apartment complex, really liked Rich and me. When the corner unit and the largest two-bedroom apartment in the complex became available she worked to convince Rich and me to move in together. Our rents would actually go down and we would have the best place in the building. The apartment had this massive living room which became party central for "our group". It had two large bedrooms and each had its own bathroom. We decided to take the nicest apartment in the building! Rich and I were like the odd couple. He loved to clean, and I liked to cook. Plus he was a neat freak and I was sort of a slob. It worked.

Donna was teaching English to eighth graders at a private school in the valley. Basically she was teaching what Donna would refer to as "Puberty English" and to the movie stars' kids. The nice part of teaching is she had summers off. Donna decided to head back east to spend some time with her folks at their Lake George summer home. Rich, my roomie decided "he" was ready and wanted to do the Palm Springs weekend. He needed some female attention and figured this crazy party in Palm Springs was just the place.

He convinced me to go with him and I figured Donna was back east, so what the hell.

We rushed out of work on Friday to beat the traffic attempting to be among the first to arrive at the Rivera Hilton. We were much too early, but we were there. Rich immediately started to drink and then drink some more as the people and women were strolling in. By midnight or so, Rich had enough, actually too much. He retreated to our room and since I was much more of a professional at this, I still had plenty of energy to dance and hang out.

I returned to our room about 2:00 AM. I opened the door and was immediately greeted by a stench that permeated out the door. I took a quick look and there was Rich, prone and not moving on the bed. The room was covered in vomit, top to bottom.

I checked him to make sure he was alive. He groaned a couple of times and I quickly left the premise. No way was I going to be able to spend the night in that room. I went out to the pool deck and grabbed a bunch of towels and made a make shift bed on some lounge chairs where I spent the rest of the night. It was plenty warm enough.

The next morning I found a maid and slipped her $20 bucks to clean up the room. Rich was alive but just barely functional. I asked him what happened and why he got so sick and he explained that he came in and had a little headache and decided to take two aspirin and go to bed. He didn't have any aspirin, so he went into my shave bag and took two from my bottle.

Now I knew the problem. Yes, I had a Tylenol bottle in my shave bag, but it didn't have Tylenol in it. It had Quaaludes. The drug that Rorer had invented as a sleeping pill which became the best barbiturate on the black market as it usually resulted in hours upon hours of great sex, if you could fight off the sleep aspect. Rich had taken two (usually a half of one was enough) and then went to bed. On top of all the alcohol he had, he was fortunate to have puked it all up. Otherwise, he may have died. Needless to say, the rest of his weekend was shot. He was a mess until Monday when it was time to head back to Van Nuys.

Rich never really recovered after that weekend and had major back issues including surgery about a year later. Donna and I had moved in together by then, but he was still a good friend to both of us. After his surgery, while laid up recovering in the hospital, we arranged with one of Donna's teacher friends to make a visit to see if she could "cheer Rich up". Betsy always liked Rich and she was happy to "accommodate" the "cheering up part".

Rich, a few weeks later confided in me that Betsy showed up with a bottle of wine and "eased his pain by taking care of another key component part of Rich's body". To this day, he thanks me for that present!

Chapter 6
GOING ALL OUT IN PALM SPRINGS/ PLAYGIRL

My weekend was much better. There were tons of people from the party scene. I really didn't want to get involved with any woman, since I was pretty involved with Donna by now. I was really just going there to keep Rich company, but he was pretty much out of the picture now.

The poolside games became the hit of the weekend. Wet t-shirt contests for the girls were entertaining and certainly plenty of drinking and smoking games. On Sunday, the girls started to complain that they were being exploited, but not the guys. They decided to do a "Best Ass" contest for the guys, where you would have to dance and shake your butt poolside while everyone else watched. Some other friends that I was hanging out with encouraged me to go for it! It was more of a dance contest, and I was a pretty good Disco-Dancer. Plus, I was feeling all loose from the party goods I had brought along.

The guys met while they went over the rules. You have to remember that the girl's wet t-shirt contest mostly ended up in "No- t-shirts" or tops, and in some cases, no bottoms contest. The guys, to a man, agreed that under no circumstance would any of us drop our bathing suits to reveal "the goods".

Contestant number one trotted out there and within two minutes, OFF CAME THE BATHING SUIT! Great, now the rest of us are either going to get booed off the poolside stage or somehow conform and peel off those shorts.

To be honest, I don't remember much about what happened poolside. I do know that at some point my shorts came down. No harm, no foul. Who's going to know anyway… Or so I thought!

That was July 4th weekend, 1978. My job with J.P. Publishers Rep Company had expanded. Fortunately, so did my salary. I was on the road much more seeing customers and selling ads. It was mid-November and I was down in Newport Beach for some sales calls and met up with an old friend from Philly who had subsequently moved out west as well. We picked a place for a quick lunch and to catch up.

I met up with Randy and the first thing he says to me is, "Do you remember my friend Sally something or other from high school?" I responded that her name sounded familiar but not really. Randy retorted, "Well she called me last night and told me that she saw my friend Harvey in PLAYGIRL MAGAZINE"! "WHAT? What are you talking about" I asked Randy. "Are you sure"? Randy reiterated to the positive and that she was 100% sure it was me.

So Randy and I headed over to the Sheraton Newport Beach sundry shop. We found the magazine section and we were kind of nervous as we were looking at the latest edition of Playgirl.

It was the December 1978 issue and we didn't want anyone to see us looking and possibly thinking we were gay or something like that. We quickly turned pages and nothing. Randy said, "She said she definitely saw you". So we went a little slower and suddenly come across an article titled: "GOING ALL OUT IN PALM SPRINGS".

I turned the page, and THERE I AM, WITH MY BATHING SUIT AROUND MY ANKLES AND IN FULL COLOR with all my "equipment" hanging out for the world to see!

Ok, I had a pretty good body in those days, but this wasn't where I wanted the world to view it. How did this happen? They never contacted me for my consent and more importantly, Donna and I had now moved in together. How was I going to explain this to her?

I bought the copy and headed back up to Los Angeles.

10 Days Prior to Breast Surgery, I returned to the Pool where the
infamous Playgirl Photo was taken- 2008

I know who could help me.... Jeff Pfizer.

I learned a ton from Jeff. After all he was a trailblazer in the magazine ad business and made a lot of money doing it. He taught me everything about that business and I had to decipher what was good and what wasn't but it was all information to utilize in my career path.

Now I needed his expertise and to see what I could do about this magazine running a nude photo in a National magazine without my consent.

Jeff directed me after a few calls to a Beverly Hills attorney. The facts were that they couldn't run it and we did have a case. But proving punitive damages would be difficult. The attorney that represented me also represented two others from that same Palm Springs party. After a few months, I was advised and agreed to settle for $7500.00. Of course my attorney took a third and Donna immediately took the remainder for herself. I may have had a case against Playgirl Magazine, but I had no case vs. my now live-in girlfriend. After all, I had talked to her throughout the weekend and told her how boring it was there in Palm Springs.

Chapter 7
BACK EAST TO NEW YORK:

I ended up working for Jeff Pfizer for almost four years and until one of the publishers I was representing wanted me to come back east and work for them directly. At first Jeff balked but then realized that Travel Agent Magazine, a thrice weekly magazine, that the travel agents relied on long before computers and their revenue, was worth a lot more than I was to him. Ironically, once I moved back to Travel Agent Magazine's corporate headquarters in New York City, Jeff now had to answer to me. I was nice and went easy on him.

During my stint in Los Angeles I met my wife Donna. We were first friends living in the same apartment complex in Van Nuys until one night when we spent the night together. The rest and the next 35 years with my "best friend" are history. Donna was also an east-coaster, moving post-college to California with some guy and then quickly breaking up. When the opportunity to move back east presented itself and we were now married, we both jumped at the chance to go. After all we saw the dark side of L.A. and didn't want to raise a family there. Many from both sides of our families questioned our marriage. I was Jewish from Philadelphia and she was an Italian from Schenectady, NY. How were we going to raise the kids? That was the question most often asked. Even our parents seemed a little split on the subject when we informed them that we were going to "tie the knot". My dad had little issue with it, especially after my grandfather, Milton, blessed the union. My mom…. well let's just say she wasn't buying in right away.

First of all she knew that any children would not be considered Jewish. Donna's folks were actually similar in their response. Her dad, who I called to ask for permission, seemed very "on board". Her mom, not so much. I think my future father in law, who had built a very successful uniform business in Schenectady and Albany, New York had some ideas that one day we might join the family business. Years later he said to me when we were actually contemplating going into their business that, "It would be nice to have a Jew in the business".

My Father-in-law had a great mind for business and was never afraid to take chances on something he felt was right for the company. My mother-in-law was the typical Italian housewife. She always had meals prepared and took care of the household while Angelo did his thing both at work and socially. A few years after we joined and opened up their 4th location in Rochester, NY, my father-in-law had a massive stroke. The family convened and we decided that I was best suited to run the company even though Donna's sister and her husband had been working for the company prior to us joining it. They kind of knew it was Angelo's wish to have the "Jew" running things. Amazingly, Angelo, although pretty much completely paralyzed on his right side and with very little speech capabilities, is still sharp with numbers and still just as stubborn as ever today. My mother-in-law has been an amazing caretaker and has catered to his every need (and believe me there are many of them) for the past 23 years. She's 84 and still going strong. She is an amazing woman to do what she has done for all of the past years.

Ok, so my mom thought I'd be back to the East Coast in four weeks after leaving for California and it was four years… but who's counting?

"Donna and Me "My Love and Best Friend for 35 years

Chapter 8
BACK TO THE DIAGNOSIS:

I realize that some of you may be wondering why this story about a man with Breast Cancer had all of this additional information about my life, especially back in the 70's. I just wanted to express that I was just like any other "kid" trying to make a mark for myself. I want the readers to know that I was just "another guy" as I matured into the working world as well as a business owner. This disease shows not boundaries and takes no prisoners. Everyone is fair game! I also found many of the former events in my life, quite interesting, or so I'm told. I wasn't the type to sit around and just "live" a normal life with a normal job in Philadelphia. I had to go see the rest of the country and try to make it on my own.

As I checked in with the receptionist at the Medical Imaging Center and presented her with the paper work from my doctor's office, she looked up at me with a little inquisitive smile and said, "So you're here for a mammogram and an ultrasound"? There might as well have been a "Giant Red Question Mark" painted on top of her entire face. After all, what was a guy doing here for a mammogram?

To her credit she tried to act nonchalant. She played the normal card as best she could, but we both knew she hadn't seen too many, if any, men checking in for a mammogram in the past. She fumbled around to give me the obligatory pre-exam paper work, normally provided to every woman coming past her window. She asked the normal questions about my insurance and history and even the phrase, "Mr. Singer, have you had a mammogram here before"?

Yea, like I've had one somewhere, anywhere else!

I took the paper work to fill out back to the waiting area. Here I sat with all of these women, filling out the obligatory paperwork. This was really when it first struck me that I was totally out of the normal in this circumstance. This was too weird to explain. How am I going to get through this process with some sort of dignity and keep my masculinity in tack?

The first page of the paper work given to me to fill out had this one third page Illustration of a naked top woman with a full frontal view. Below this was an additional one third page Illustration of a naked top woman with a side view. My job was to draw in where my lump was and any other abnormalities of my breast!

The illustration showed a woman with estimated "C" Cups. Now this may have been fun to look at when I was 10 or 12 years old, but right now it was downright uncomfortable. I, like all of the women in the waiting area, are drawing in pictures on our breasts, prior to having a mammogram. In school I could look over to the next desk and copy or cheat some answers. That wasn't going to work for me right now.

On the next page I was asked all of the other "normal" questions prior to getting a mammogram.

Am I or could I be pregnant? (**NOPE, I Don't think so!**)
When was the date of my last period? (**Hmmm… how's Never?**)
Have I ever had excessive bleeding during my period? (**See Above.**)
When was my last gynecological visit and Pap smear? (**Probably, right after my last period.**)
Do I have Implants? If so, what kind and when were they done? (**I have a part that could certainly use an implant**)

I remember thinking couldn't they have just eliminated these pages and given me the ones that made sense for a man to fill in? I kept looking over to see if any woman sitting around me actually saw me drawing in the area of my lump on this "C" cup breast. What could they possibly be thinking?

After what seemed to be forever, my named was called. I walked slowly and deliberately following the nurse technician to the back area. I was given a patient gown to change into and instructed to put the "opening" to the front. This was different. Every other time I've been in one of these ridiculous patient gowns, I was told to leave the opening in the back.

I was directed toward the room that contained the mysterious "Mammogram X Ray Machine". I, like most guys, had never seen one of these contraptions. I was instructed as to where to stand and wondered how in the world they were going to get my little tit into a position where they can actually get a good X-ray of it.

These two large, clamp like things, came down and grabbed about as much of my chest skin as they could muster. The machine was closed down, squeezing my already sore left breast into a metal sandwich and I was told to "HOLD STILL" while they left and snapped endless amounts of X-ray photos from a nearby room.

The tech returned to perform a similar circumstance to my right breast. This was much easier as the right side was not sore, nor was I mentally worried about the outcome of those photos.

Next they moved me into another room with a flat table and this paddle type machine just to the right of the table. This, I was informed, was to look at the area in question via ultra sound. A half liquid half gel type solution was spread out of what looked like a squeeze type ketchup or mustard container on the area. The ultra sound machine's paddle was then moved circularly around the area for about five to seven minutes. No pain here, it actually felt soothing. And so was the technician performing the task. She was young, cute and seemed to sense my worry and concern. She attempted to be very comforting by her conversation in response to my situation.

She left the room but I remained behind. Approximately 10 minutes later, the door opened and a doctor appeared. She was the radiologist on staff and introduced herself being sure to also announce some of her credentials. I guess this was to assure me that she was in fact a full doctor and not another technician working the machines.

The radiologist explained to me that there was definitely a "mass" directly under my left nipple and proceeded to show me the film from the mammogram. She then flipped over to the films from the ultra sound, explaining that the mass wasn't "fluid" filled and was obviously "calcified". When I asked for further explanation, she told me that "fluid" would not be of concern and more likely be a cyst of some sort. Calcification indicates a more detailed problem, that doesn't necessarily mean cancer, but certainly could be. When I questioned what the odds were that this mass would be cancerous, she looked at me hesitantly and stated "50/50". Somehow I read her eyes and facial expression and wasn't buying the 50/50 part. Maybe I was just being more paranoid, but as a salesperson for my entire working life, you learn how to read people and their expressions. You have to be able to read people and have to be fairly accurate as facial expressions allow you to be a successful salesperson. They tell you when to turn up the pressure to close a deal or when to back down and take a more conservative means to the end.

I then looked over at the "tech" that was still accompanying the doctor in the room. She had followed me throughout the testing process and I could definitely see through her expressions and body language that she was concerned for me. The radiologist then told me that my next step was to have a biopsy done on the mass to find out for sure what it was.

I was already pretty sure what it was.

It was Breast Cancer!

It was late in the afternoon on a Friday. What the hell was I going to do with this knowledge so late in the day on a Friday?

Just for a bit more medical information: Not ALL male breast lumps are cancerous. Men can have breast lumps and they can be painful and still not be cancerous. These benign lumps are called "Gynecomastia". They tend to show up around the time a young man goes through puberty, although they can be formed or detected at any age.

According to the SUSAN G. KOMEN FOUNDATION:

Gynecomastia results from a hormone imbalance in the body. Certain diseases, hormone use, obesity and other hormone changes can cause this imbalance. For example, boys can get a temporary form of gynecomastia during puberty.

Gynec`omastia does not need to be treated unless it is desired or it causes pain. In these cases, it can be treated with hormone therapy or surgery. At this time it is unclear whether gynecomastia is related to breast cancer. Although some data suggest it may increase the risk of breast cancer in men, most studies have found no link between the two.

WHAT DO I DO NEXT?

Oddly enough, my first call upon leaving the imaging office was not to my wife, who I knew was waiting to hear from me. My mind was going a thousand miles per hour and I needed to know what my next step was. As I was driving out of the parking lot, I reached for my cell phone and called my little sister, Vicki.

Thirteen years prior, Vicki was diagnosed with breast cancer at the ripe old age of 36, one month after my mother Libby was diagnosed with breast cancer! Pretty fucking shocking when your baby sister and your mom are diagnosed with the same dreaded disease one month apart.

After our mom was diagnosed, Vicki decided to insist on a mammogram, even though protocol usually states that at 40, women should start to have their first mammograms. She had the intuition that it may be genetic and she just wanted to be sure.

My mom had a lumpectomy followed by radiation in that year, 1995. Vicki had a lumpectomy and did not require radiation as a follow up. Three or so years later, Vicki's cancer resurfaced.

Another lumpectomy was performed. Several years later another routine follow up visit to the oncologist showed another cancerous mass in her breast. Against all the doctors' recommendations, Vicki refused to have a mastectomy. Most women would not agree, but she chose to keep both of her natural breasts.

Vicki and her husband Gary were about as well versed on breast cancer as anyone. Gary is by trade a pharmacist, as was his father. Together and then mostly through Gary's hard work, intellect and dedication, they prospered by building a small regional drugstore into a chain of big pharmacy and discount health stores. Not long before my sister's first diagnosis of breast cancer, Gary sold off his stores and after a short stint working for the new owners, went back into business as a natural health and supplement retailer.

It was quite the venture, utilizing his original building in a northeastern suburb about 30 miles from Philadelphia. This store had more vitamins and supplements than I had ever seen under one roof. He had a holistic center upstairs which offered massage and other therapeutic services. Gary is one of the smartest people I have ever met. A bit of a tyrant in business and can be almost verbally degrading at times. But brilliant!

He began to read and attend seminars and learn every aspect of the holistic world of health care. If there existed a natural supplement in the universe that he did not know about, it would have been news. Organic foods became the only thing allowed into their home. They constantly and subtly pushed Donna and my family more toward supplements and toward more organic foods in our home. While raising my two boys, both who were extremely athletic and prominent athletes in our community, Gary would send me supplements to help them succeed and maximize their potential.

Customers would come into Gary's store and pay large amounts of money to meet with Gary privately to explain to him what their health issues were. Gary would then do some testing and analysis and prescribe a regimen of supplements which he would subsequently sell to them. I often joked to them that this was quite the racket. They pay you to listen and prescribe all of these vitamins and supplements that you sell to them!

No one cared because in most cases they worked. Having the pharmaceutical background and then knowing pretty much all there is to know about the holistic supplement world was quite the unique combination. Gary knew when natural supplements couldn't or wouldn't do the job and when traditional medicine needed to be administered. Gary would never jeopardize a client's health just to sell additional supplements. In some cases, his regimens were able to succeed when modern day medicine failed.

Today, you can attend a specific Nature-Path Medical school. Vicki and Gary's son, my nephew Jeremy is just completing his schooling out in Arizona to become a Nature-Path Doctor. He can do everything that any other doctor can do or prescribe, but has the additional education in natural vitamins and supplements as well as homeopathic medicine. Not every state recognizes Nature-Path's, but the number is growing on a regular basis.

This is how Vicki and Gary attacked Vicki's breast cancer. They knew pretty much every aspect and every form of treatment available. Gary also knew all the detriments of today's medical treatments for breast cancer and many of them, including chemotherapy, were not very high up on his list. They both knew that once Vicki went through radiation oncology treatments, that option was off the table. You couldn't do it again. The next step would have to be chemo or something else drastic.

It wasn't until Vicki's third bout with breast cancer and it was a little more involved that she opted to have another lumpectomy followed by radiation. Still no mastectomy! Still no chemotherapy!

After Vicki's third diagnosis of malignancy, she went through the very expensive and tedious process of genetic testing. Because she and our mom were both diagnosed a month apart, in addition to our mom's sister, several years before, Vicki was determined to find out the root cause if possible. There were also my mom's two brothers who had both died of some form of cancer. No one knew for sure what kind of cancer as this was in the late 1940's.

I remember her calling me after obtaining the results from her testing and informing me that she was in fact, a carrier of the BRCA 2 Gene Mutation. She said to me that I should consider getting tested as well and that not only was I at risk, but so could my two sons be at risk.

But why would I be of risk for breast cancer?

I'm not a female and I don't really have breasts. Nor do my two boys. After questioning her about me and the why of it, she never really discussed the breast cancer issue exactly, leaning more toward discussing other aspects of this genetic flaw. Things like being more prone for early-onset prostate cancer were discussed as were some other cancerous predispositions. In my mind, I was like, well ok, whatever. I'll take it under advisement. Maybe someday I'll look into it. Vicki brought it back up several times over the next few years, usually just in a suggestive forum. She was never being that adamant or overly assertive in her conversations with me. It just wasn't her style to be too demanding. After all she was my younger sister and knows me well enough to know that I hardly ever listen to anyone with whom I disagreed.

So on this crucial day in my life, I reached out to the one person who knew me the best and who knows more about this disease than any other regular person.

This is why my first call was to my sister. She certainly would offer me the most reinforcement emotionally and the most information educationally. After all, she had lived it for the past 14 years.

She seemed surprised, extremely concerned and very much saddened by the information I was relaying to her. She wasn't shocked! This surprised me a little, but her knowledge of the BRCA2 gene and the potential that I too, could be a carrier, probably left a hardened and informed mark on her brain. I wasn't shocked that I could be a carrier and potentially have prostate or some other form of cancer. But I never expected that I, a man, could have breast cancer.

Even though I had been living with noted and recognizable symptoms for about three months, I never put my sister's issues, her BRCA 2 positive and my concerns together. Not once did Breast Cancer cross my mind.

Never!

"The Four of Us" in St. Maarten.

Chapter 9
BRCA 2

Many have heard of BRCA 1 and BRCA 2 but most know nothing about it except for the fact that if you're carrying the BRCA mutation, there is a much higher probability of contracting breast cancer. That's all I knew besides the fact that my sister and probably my mom were both carriers.

According to the National Cancer Institute:
BRCA1 and BRCA2 are human genes that belong to a class of genes known as tumor suppressors.

*In normal cells, BRCA 1 and BRCA 2 help ensure the stability of the cell's genetic material (DNA) and help prevent uncontrolled cell growth. Mutation of these genes has been linked to the development of hereditary breast and ovarian cancer. The names **BRCA1** and **BRCA2** stand for **Breast Cancer susceptibility gene 1 and Breast Cancer susceptibility gene 2, respectively.***

Not all gene changes or mutations are harmful. Some mutations may be beneficial whereas others may have no obvious effect or be neutral. Harmful mutations can increase a person's risk of developing a disease, such as cancer.

A woman's lifetime risk of developing breast and/or ovarian cancer is greatly increased if she inherits a harmful mutation in BRCA1 or BRCA2. Such a woman has an increased risk of developing breast and/ or ovarian cancer at an early age, (before menopause) and often has multiple, close family members who have been diagnosed with these diseases. Harmful BRCA1 mutations may also increase a woman's risk of developing cervical, uterine, pancreatic, and colon cancer. Harmful BRCA2 mutations may additionally increase the risk of pancreatic cancer, stomach cancer, gallbladder and bile duct cancers as well as melanoma.

MEN with harmful BRCA1 mutations also have an increased risk of breast cancer and possibly of pancreatic cancer, testicular cancer and early-onset prostate cancer. However male breast cancer, pancreatic cancer and prostate cancer appear to be more strongly associated with BRCA2 gene mutations!

Ashkenazi Jews (those of Central and Eastern European family descent) are at a higher risk than those in the average population.

According to estimates from the National Cancer Institute, the lifetime risk is about 12% of women in the general population to develop breast cancer sometime during their lives compared with about 60% who have inherited the harmful BRCA1 or BRCA2 mutation. This means a woman's chance is about five times more likely to develop breast cancer if they have the BRCA harmful mutation.

The percentage of men who have the "harmful" BRCA1 or BRCA2 mutation have only about a 6.5% chance of developing breast cancer but have about a 70% chance of developing early on-set prostate cancer! (I have had both 18 months apart!)

There are also additional factors that have much to do with how many other family members have developed these cancers and there the numbers multiply.

Just recently, before publication of this book, Angelina Jolie the very famous movie actress and wife of Brad Pitt wrote into the NY Times Op-Ed section to claim that she recently underwent a preventative or prophylactic bi-lateral mastectomy. She provided her details and decision for undergoing such a brave move. Her mom had recently passed away at the age of 60 from Ovarian Cancer. The cancer was a product of her being BRCA positive. Angelina subsequently had BRCA Genetic Testing and found out that she also was carrying the BRCA 1 Gene Mutation. In an effort to stave off (what "she estimated" as 80%) her chance of contracting breast cancer she made this courageous decision. She also stated that she will, subsequently at a later date, have her ovaries removed in an effort to avoid ovarian cancer as well.

Suddenly BRCA, which I have and most people know little about, became front page news! Angelina had used her celebrity status to now educate millions of people about BRCA and its detriment to our society.

I applaud Angelina for being brave, publicizing her decision and making people aware. What I found very disturbing was throughout all the National and International coverage this decision received, including every major TV news outlet and every newspaper and weekly magazine, never once did I see, hear or read that the BRCA mutation can be carried by a MAN as well.

NOT ONCE!

There are just as many men who carry the BRCA Genetic Mutation, yet because Breast Cancer is associated only with females, no one even mentions these facts. BRCA Mutations can be given from a man to his daughter, from a woman to his son, from a woman to her daughter or from a man to his son. No sexual discrimination here!

All of this coverage to make women aware and never once mentioning that a man can have BRCA and will likely get some form of cancer from it, is total sexual discrimination at its root and is a just another fight that I am taking on.

Insurance companies treat men with BRCA and subsequent breast cancer differently. Many won't allow for reconstruction or even screening on a regular basis. THIS NEEDS TO CHANGE!

Additionally, many new cancer drug therapies are being tested that actually repair the mutated gene and can even reverse active cancers in our bodies. Slowly but surely we're getting to the point where we are no longer controlled by the medical world, the insurance companies and especially the drug companies in our fight to survive these types of cancers.

In my case, my mom, as well as my mom's sister, are both breast cancer survivors. My mom's two brothers who both passed away at a very early age, were diagnosed with some form of cancer, but we will never know if they were carrying the BRCA2 mutation that Vicki and I carry. We do know that our older brother Jeff has been tested and is also a carrier, but to this point, thankfully, has had no cancer diagnosis.

Vicki and I as well as Jeff have a 50/50 chance that we have passed along the ***BRCA2 harmful mutation*** to each of our 8 children. (All of our children are boys except for one girl, my brother's daughter Ashley) BRCA2 is not just a woman's issue!

In addition to Ashkenazi Jews there are other ethnic and geographic populations around the world who have a higher concentration of BRCA1 and BRCA2 harmful mutations. These include Norwegian, Dutch and Icelandic peoples.

The determining test is basically a blood test that takes a couple of weeks to create accurate results. Those individuals who decide to get tested have to be counseled on the potential results and the ramifications of these results as they have major psychological risks associated with them.

Myriad, the drug company that discovered the BRCA Gene has held a patent on the gene and its diagnostic testing. Just a few weeks before publication of this book, the U.S. Supreme Court ruled that Myriad no longer could hold the patent on a gene that is part of our body and that other companies will soon be allowed to do the testing as well. This "should" bring the costs for the BRCA test down, as there will now be competition. This, I perceive as a huge victory in the fight to identify BRCA carriers. Ultimately, it should also pressure the insurance companies to pay for screenings for men at high risk as well as for women. Currently, this is not the case.

I chose to have the testing to insure I knew what and where my cancer emanated from. My boys know that they have the ability to test as well but they have to be prepared for the results, either positive or negative. In the interim, they are aware that they "could be" and they should be much more aware of any changes in their bodies.

Since BRCA2 harmful mutation can cause breast, prostate or pancreatic cancer, I choose to be screened with the most state of the art testing methods available. Recently I had a new screening test for pancreatic cancer. This is called an "Endoscopic Ultrasound". To date it's the most comprehensive test available to screen the pancreas. Pancreatic cancer is extremely deadly mostly because by the time it "presents" any symptoms it has usually spread to other organs. The control rate for pancreatic cancer survival is very low, about 6% according to most studies. There is no absolute cure at this time.

There is so much more involved with the BRCA1 and BRCA2 mutations and only a true geneticist would really understand it all. I can only say that it is associated with the 13th chromosome and the true name is BRCA2 –Early Onset, and you should pray that you don't carry it.

I don't think I'm alone. Most men, frankly most women, simply don't ever associate breast cancer with men. It's just not that common and almost never talked about. Even the doctors, oncologists and radiological offices don't provide for the possibility of it occurring. Remember those forms I had to complete?

Vicki and I talked for most of my trip home. We were both composed and calm for each other. I was just seeking direction as to what to do next.

First my regular doctor, who I did trust even though he had only been with this practice for about 18 months, was gone. I certainly wasn't going to put a lot of confidence in a Physician's Assistant to guide me. Vicki advised me that the first thing I needed to do was to find the most competent breast surgeon possible. She told me not to settle for a regular surgeon and instead find someone here in Rochester who specializes in Breast Cancer Surgery. She doubted that I would find anyone who specialized in male breast cancer surgery.

Because the calcification was considered "smaller" she was fairly confident that I found it early enough to have a lumpectomy done and that barring any infiltration into my lymph nodes, the process would go smoothly and I would be fine. Some of this conversation I sensed as true, other parts I deemed her attempting to comfort my fears.

Seconds later, I was back on the phone calling my wife to fill her in as I knew she was waiting anxiously to hear from me. Here the emotions got the best of me. I was able to keep myself sort of composed with Vicki, but once I began talking to my wife the reality of the situation came crashing down on me. Speaking with Donna, my mind reverted to our two boys and all of the "What Ifs?"

Our boys are all grown up. They're both great kids who were successful academically and athletically as well. Matthew earned a packaging engineering degree from RIT (Rochester Institute of Technology), where he was also a standout centerfielder and lead-off hitter for the RIT Tiger's baseball team. He was living in North Central California and working as a packaging and quality control engineer for a major winery.

Jameson, two years his younger, followed in my footsteps, obtaining a Journalism degree from Quinnipiac University in Connecticut and was and still is, chasing his dream of being a professional player as well as a journalist in the thriving poker industry.

At this crossroads time in my life, I was still very concerned not only for me, but for the trauma I was about to have my entire family endure. Cancer is as much of a battle for the families as it is for the patient himself. I had heard that before, I just couldn't believe I was experiencing it myself. Adding to that mix were the thoughts that my boys may be at risk and you can get an idea of what Donna and I were going through.

Donna and I talked about a course of action and reaction. We were in business together in her family's uniform business for 22 years. Three and half years earlier, we had sold off the catalog division of our business to a large manufacturer and supplier. I left as part of the deal to work directly for the manufacturer for a minimum of five years.

One of the largest accounts we handled on the local level remained with Uniform Village and Donna was now running the company in Rochester. This account was the largest and most important teaching hospital and university in all of Upstate New York, The University of Rochester Medical Center and Strong Memorial Hospital. Since my departure from the "family" business, Donna handles almost all of the hospital's uniform needs, including all of the scrubs for almost every department. She also supplies most of the lab coats worn by the physicians, as well as all of the GME (Graduate Medical Education) lab coats, that cover the residents working non-stop at the hospital, in addition to many other departments.

Strong was also the most prolific cancer treatment center, by far, in Rochester. The new Wilmot Cancer Center had just recently opened about eight months earlier.

Listening to my sister's suggestions to find "the best breast cancer surgeon possible", I asked Donna to start calling over to any close contact she had and see what she could dig up regarding the most renowned breast cancer surgeon. She was able to reach two key contacts at Strong Hospital and they each pointed to the same two surgeons.

The first was Dr. Stephanie Connors. Dr. Connors was both an oncologist and surgeon and one of the directors of Strong's breast cancer unit. The other was Dr. Chris Samuelson, who worked with a very reputable surgical group and out of several different Rochester area hospitals.

I immediately began searching on-line to see what I could find out about both noted surgeons.

The amazing thing about the internet today is that you can virtually research anything and everyone. Doctors are especially easy to research online. There are multiple websites that offer patient feedback and reviews of any doctor. Any! You can also Google the physician and find all of the articles he or she has authored. Plus any noted awards or other types of recognition may show up on line.

I'm not exactly sure why but my thoughts immediately gravitated toward Dr. Samuelson. I think my predisposition toward female doctors combined with having a "woman's" disease and being treated by a woman, sort of pointed me in that direction. Both doctors received nothing but high marks on all of my web based research. Speed became of the essence to me, as I was definitely in panic mode.

Remember, I still didn't really have a firm diagnosis. Only a biopsy was going to positively identify this calcified mass, but I was sure! And I wasn't going to sit idly by and wait to hear it officially before seeking out the best possible care. I needed to be proactive. To this day I preach being proactive when it comes to your own healthcare. Doctors are all just too busy and very overworked. Patients can just fall to the side if you don't insure that you are on top of their "to-do" lists.

I spent that night researching everything about male breast cancer I could find on the web. Believe me, there wasn't that much available. Almost every article, every website, every single item I could bring up said the same thing. "Male breast cancer mimics female breast cancer and is treated the same way". That was it. That's all they had to say about it.

I did find a couple of websites, posted by families of men who had breast cancer and had since passed away. This… didn't exactly make me feel much better about what may have been coming. The American Cancer Society says that the mortality rate of male breast cancer patients is fairly similar to the mortality rate for females. The only problem is that men tend to ignore, for much longer, the initial symptoms. Many times, by the time they actually get their symptoms checked, the cancer is far more advanced, metastasized or already spread to the lymph nodes or other areas. Then, the mortality rates are higher. Most women are screened regularly and know how to self-examine. Not men. Men are not screened and just tend to ignore the warning signs because they don't expect breast cancer to form in their bodies.

Much of the information I could find indicated that the precise area where my lump was located, was exactly where most men's cancerous tumors form. This area, right below or beside the nipple, was almost always malignant. Nipple indentation is another warning sign. This was just another confirmation of my worst fear as I had both.

After a night of virtually little or no sleep and a lot of tossing and turning, I spent Saturday morning doing more research on line and attempting to figure out what my next step would be. On-line research can be hazardous to your mental health. The more I read, the more scared I became. TMI! Too much information about medical conditions is not a good thing. Yes, you want and need to be informed, but you have to know when to stop reading. Unfortunately, that Friday night into the wee hours of Saturday morning, I couldn't stop or hold myself back from continuing to read and research. Hell, I wasn't going to sleep anyway, so why not stay busy.

I decided that I had to figure out a way to get in to see Dr. Samuelson as soon as possible. I had to get this thing out of my body… YESTERDAY! I couldn't bear walking around knowing that this cancer was growing inside of me. It was consuming every second of my mental makeup. Donna kept saying to me that on Monday, one of her contacts at Strong Hospital would help me get in quickly.

I was growing impatient and didn't even want to wait until Monday. Who do I know and what could I do? My primary doctor was gone and I was dealing with an office that has become almost socialized, more like a clinic than a true personal doctor's office. I needed another alternative.

My Son Jameson at the World Series of Poker, 2010

My Son Matthew with my Sister Vicki in 2012

Chapter 10
ONE GREAT DOCTOR

From 1977 until 1985 I had battled colitis. A horrible condition that affects your lower bowel causing bouts of diarrhea accompanied by cramping then constipation, and terrible gastro intestinal discomfort. It had affected me off and on for over eight years all while living in Los Angeles, Princeton, NJ and then after we moved to Upstate, New York.

My colitis was another wonderful genetic present passed along to me from my mom, who suffered immensely from it throughout most of my early childhood. My brother and I remember many visits to the hospital to see her and then when she returned home, watching her grind up steak or chicken into almost a liquid, in order to eat. No one ever seemed to be able to figure out how to treat her or how to help her. In the 1960's I guess they figured that if your food was almost in a digested form by the time it reached your large intestines, that the colitis condition would have an easier time and it would be less stressful for the colon to handle the digestive process. It didn't work.

Ulcerative Colitis means that your colon forms these small ulcers throughout the large intestine. When food passes through this area, it irritates or aggravates these ulcers and causes them to bleed and to distress your entire bowel system. Colitis is sometimes confused with Irritable Bowel Syndrome (IBS). They present similar symptoms both of which are literally a "pain in the ass" and stomach.

I had seen numerous doctors in three different cities who attempted to diagnose me and find a way to treat me. None of them succeeded until I met Dr. Bob Greenfield.

Dr. Greenfield was able to ascertain that I did in fact have ulcerative colitis and after almost a year of treatment, was able to silence the horrible symptoms that accompanied my flare ups. I did endure some subsequent episodes over those first few years, but for the most part his treatment was able to arrest my condition. I had not had a real colitis flare up since about 1988 or so, but I would still see Dr. Greenfield every year and have a colonoscopy every 18 months. Believe me he knows my rectum better than anyone!

We've always had a very good patient to doctor relationship. Doc's a huge New York Giants fan, since I'm a diehard Eagles fan, we would spend most visits talking more football than medical health issues. We both like to gamble a little on sports and he also dabbles a little in the world of poker, much like my younger son. I always thought of Dr. Greenfield as a friend as well as my most competent doctor.

On this Saturday morning, as I sat and pondered a way of getting in to see a surgeon as soon as possible, I decided that Dr. Greenfield may be my answer. I couldn't possibly reach him on a Saturday, could I? I would probably have to wait until Monday morning to do so.

After thinking it through a little further, I remembered that he almost always did procedures on Monday morning, and this would cause me to not be able to reach him until at least Monday afternoon, if at all.

I know I'm just another patient to most of the doctors with whom I have visited with over the years, but I also knew that after 20 years, if I called him, even on a Saturday and left word, he just may call me back.

I gave it a shot.

I called his office and of course was redirected to the answering service. I left word that I needed to speak with him as soon as possible, never really stating what my issue was. Twenty minutes later my phone rang and the voice on the other end said, "Hey Harvey, its Dr. Greenfield. What's up?"

I began to tell Dr. Greenfield that "I had breast cancer". I didn't say, I thought I had it, or it was likely I had breast cancer. I just said "I have breast cancer". His reaction was not very comforting to me as he responded with, "Oh my God". At this point I said to him, "well that's great, you're a doctor. You're not supposed to respond like that". "You just caught me off-guard", he said. "You just don't expect to hear that from a guy".

Even my closest doctor knows this isn't supposed to be happening to me.

After a couple of minutes of me explaining what had transpired over the past 24 hours and regarding my symptoms, he asked me what he could do to help. This is when I brought up the name of Dr. Samuelson and if he possibly knew him and if he could help me get in to see him quickly. Dr. Samuelson's reputation being what it is as a renowned surgeon, meant a minimum of three to four weeks to get an appointment. When I posed his name to Dr. Greenfield, his response blew me away. "Yes, I know him well. Matter of fact I'm at the hospital right now making rounds and I just passed him 10 minutes ago in the hallway. Let me see if I can find him and I'll call you back".

Within 10 minutes my phone rang again and Dr. Greenfield said to me, "You're all set. I just spoke with Dr. Samuelson and you just need to call his office first thing Monday morning and they'll set you up". He concluded by giving me his personal cell phone and advised me that if I needed anything, anything at all, to call him. Now that's a caring doctor. That's a friend!

I spoke with Dr. Samuelson's office first thing on Monday morning. After a couple of back and forth phone calls, with little conversation, the office finally did in fact confirm that Dr. Greenfield and Dr. Samuelson had "discussed me". Physicians and especially surgeons are funny. They never seem to show the urgency or demeanor of concern that we patients have. I am certain that this is process of "everyday medicine". They never get too involved or too close to a patient and never make anything seem like it's an emergency.

By Monday afternoon I was able to get Dr. Samuelson's office to schedule a "rushed" biopsy for me. Remember, through this whole process,

NOTHING was yet confirmed medically. Only my own mindset had this diagnosis locked in. Dr. Samuelson was not going to meet with me until the biopsy results were back and the cancer was confirmed.

They arranged my wonderful visit to the large Imaging Center for Tuesday, subsequently setting up an appointment with Dr. Samuelson, the only appointment available, which just happened to be on Thursday. Thursday was Yom Kippur, the holiest day of the year for the Jewish faith.

All Jewish Holidays begin at sundown and end the next day after the sun goes down. Yom Kippur is the "Day of Atonement". This is the day when all practicing Jews ask for God's forgiveness for all of their sins from the year before and look to go into the New Year with a clean slate.

Practicing Catholics can relate to it as "confession". Where Catholics go to confession and sit across from a priest and confess their sins and then ask for forgiveness, the Jewish faith has one day a year where the entire group of religious followers band together in Synagogues and ask for our forgiveness for all of the bad things we did in the year before. Even confessions we do at "wholesale", once a year rather than several times per year for the Catholics.

I remember thinking, "I guess I must have done some really terrible things to get this sentence passed down on this day".

I am fairly "Jew Light", as my friends will tell you. I married out of the faith to an Italian girl. We both have strong family traditions which the Jews and Italians have in common and our families are more important to us than the religious aspects of our faith. Italians and Jews are similar, except the FOOD is much better on the Italian side! (with the exception of my mom's Kamish bread! Some call it Mondel Bread)

Being married to an Italian girl for the past 33 years and raising our two boys fairly non-religious, but with an investment in God, I am not considered a practicing Jew. I love being Jewish and I love my heritage, but I don't go to synagogue regularly or very much at all. Only for weddings or family Bar Mitzvah's or once in a while if I'm back in Philadelphia for the high holidays, do I set foot in a synagogue or temple.

The one holiday I always attempt to keep is Yom Kippur. After all, it is the "Day of Forgiveness". "The Day of Atonement". To ask for forgiveness, Jews are asked to fast and to not eat or drink anything from sundown to sundown on this holy day. We should be in Synagogue praying for God's forgiveness or at least asking and laying low at home. In the old days you couldn't even drive a car or watch TV on this day. My grandfather, Milton, dispelled much of the old culture when he had a conflict between going to synagogue or watching the World Series on television. He found a way to watch the game. I guess in the old days, cars were deemed as a luxury item and not a necessity item, so we were to walk to services.

Since I was Bar Mitzvah at 13 years old, I have always fasted and kept this holiday according to tradition. Something about it being a "day of forgiveness" was always very prominent for me. I guess I have enough sins throughout the year to atone for!

When Dr. Samuelson's office instructed me that the ONLY day they could get me in that week was Thursday, Yom Kippur, I didn't even hesitate. It's funny how things change their perspective when you feel vulnerable to death. They also insisted that I have the biopsy before my visit with the doctor.

I did the biopsy. It wasn't the worst procedure I had ever been through from a physical pain perspective. It was much more of mental anguish, knowing the results that were forthcoming.

I received that dreaded but expected call on Yom Kippur evening.

I HAD BREAST CANCER!

I guess I wasn't really surprised, but it still struck me hard, none the less.

The next day my wife and I went to visit the surgeon and to discuss what the results confirmed. Now we had to find out what was to be our next step.

After a full exam with the surgical Physician's Assistant, Beverly and an involved and lengthy meeting with Dr. Samuelson, I was relieved on some fronts, and shocked on others.

First of all, the smaller size of the tumor that had been noted on most accounts by the professionals advising me was fairly accurate. Between one and two centimeters was a good sign. This size indicated a less likelihood of having the cancer spreading into the lymph nodes or metastasized. Nothing guaranteed but "less likely". Did you ever notice how medical professionals NEVER GUARANTEE ANYTHING? They can't. That's why they call it "PRACTICING" medicine.

The biggest shock to us that day was that the lumpectomy, my sister had had four times, and the procedure I was most expecting, considering the size of the tumor and acknowledged by all of the WOMEN who have dealt with this disease, WAS OFF THE BOARD!

"WHY?" was what my wife and I both asked of the surgeon in unison?

Once again, a **"Man with a Woman's Disease"** was the difference.

The answer is: Because in a man, there's not enough breast tissue to remove just the tumor (lump) and have clean margins. By the time you remove the tumor and all the surrounding possibly infiltrated tissue, there's not any real tissue left to work with.

Nope, I was informed I needed to have a full mastectomy. My entire left breast would need to be removed.

"My entire left breast", I asked?

"Yes", was my doctor's response! "Including your nipple and areola area around your nipple"

I remember thinking to myself, "What the hell is that going to look like? I'm going to look like a freak!"

I got past it.

Look, the only thing that really mattered to me and should matter was that I needed to get rid of this cancer and LIVE ON.

Dr. Samuelson and his P.A. (Physician's Assistant) both were quite calm and comforting and assured my wife and me that all things would work out fine. The tumor was fairly small and they saw no indication that spreading had occurred. Although there was a chance that the tumor had spread into my lymph system, they seemed to be assured that most likely it had not.

We talked about a time frame for surgery. I come from the school of, "Ok let's go. When can I have the surgery? Tomorrow? Next Monday? A Week from Today?"

As I soon discovered it was a little more complicated than that. I needed to have some additional tests run, including all of the normal pre-surgery work ups by the hospital.

In addition I needed to have, the day before surgery, a nuclear dye injected into the tumor. This nuclear dye would then be followed by a specific nuclear X-ray and they would follow it until it would ultimately gravitate to what is known as the "Sentinel Node". This, I was totally unaware of. But, hey, it seems like I'm learning something new every day.

The object of this test is to locate the first lymph node most likely to be infiltrated by the cancer. The day of surgery the first thing to be done to me once inside the operating room, and under anesthesia, was the removal of this "Sentinel Lymph node".

Upon removal, they would rush the node off to pathology, while they went to work extracting the tumor and surrounding tissues. Ultimately, by the time they had completed surgically removing my entire left breast tissue the pathology report would be back and they would know whether or not the cancer had moved into my lymph system. If the lymph node came back positive for cancer, they would proceed to remove ALL OF MY LYMPH NODES!

To me this was one of my biggest fears going into the surgery. I wasn't all that afraid of having surgery. I wasn't all that scared of being a "One-Tit-Man" upon waking up. I never really feared all the possible circumstances and problems the hospital and anesthesiologist make you sign wavers about during the pre-op consultation. Nope, none of that really bothered me too much. I've had surgery before. Just another one in the books.

What I feared most, was awaking to find the results of that sentinel node biopsy. I knew that a POSITIVE NODE was going to mean a LOT MORE NEGATIVES FOR ME!

The surgeon informed me in our consultation that it would take about 3-4 weeks or so, to get everything scheduled. I remember thinking, "THREE OR FOUR WEEKS"? What the hell? I'm walking around with this tumor, this cancer in my chest, and you want me to wait THREE TO FOUR WEEKS? Just get it the fuck out of me!

Dr. Samuelson sensed my frustration and concern. I guess he's "been there, done that" with many other patients before. He was very calming and assured me that a few weeks, was NOT GOING to change anything. As much as I would have liked to believe all he was telling me, there was still something going through my brain, saying "get it the fuck out, NOW"!

He told me that this cancer had probably been growing in me for some five to seven years. Maybe more. Another couple of weeks were not going to change anything or ultimately alter the outcome to my health. My wife and I explained that we had a vacation planned to Palm Desert with a group of couples and had planned this for almost eight months. I didn't care about the trip, and I would happily have cancelled it for us, if I could have the surgery earlier. The doc looked at me and said point blank: "GO. Go on your vacation and have a great time. Try not to think about your disease."

Yea, OK! (easy to say, not so easy to do)

As it turned out, somehow, I was able to go away and "sort of" put my issues to the side. Not behind me, but just off to the side. The doctor had at least alleviated my critical concerns for LIFE vs. DEATH, for the time being. He assured Donna and me that I would ultimately be fine and most likely need very little follow up treatment. Treatments such as chemotherapy or radiation, were very unlikely.

He did think I would need a form of hormone therapy. Taxmoxifen was the name I kept hearing. As he called it, "just a pill, that I would have to take daily for the next several years".

I remember thinking, "OK, I can live with that". Surgery with a six week recovery period and a pill once a day for the next five years and voila', I have my life back.

These positive thoughts enabled me to actually go on this long planned vacation and although I knew I was facing surgery and who knows what else, I was going to go and enjoy myself.

Remember the Philly Boyz group of guys I referred to earlier? This trip was with many of the Philly Boyz, only this time, for the first time, we were going with our wives as couples. A week in the perfect climate of Palm Desert, CA with 12 of us! Good Friends. Good Times, Good Golf and GREAT DINNERS!

THE PHILLY BOYZ & GIRLZ-2008

In the middle of that week, our beloved Philadelphia Phillies, would be opening up Game #1 of the 2008 World Series in Tampa Bay against the surprisingly upstart Tampa Rays.

What a fabulous week we had, including the opening night party at my place, where we brought in some food and made some additional items in house. I made my classic guacamole, a fan favorite whenever I go to a party. Many times people ONLY invite me to their parties to ensure I will arrive bearing my infamous recipe. Of course alcoholic beverage of choice go hand in hand with the guacamole. Tequila Margaritas! Another special recipe of mine, devised over the years of my travel in the restaurant business.

(I'll divulge both recipes at the end of this book)

We went on the trip. My friends all knew of my diagnosis by now. Mostly they avoided the subject and spent the week like nothing was wrong.

Lots of golf and great dinners out. The highlight for me came on the day we went to Palm Springs to take a high-wire tram up the mountain and hike through their mountains. After the hike we grabbed a quick lunch in downtown Palm Springs. This is when I realized that we were only a couple of blocks away from the hotel that used to be the Palm Springs Rivera Hilton. It was now just called the Rivera. About six of us went over to the hotel. It had been completely refurbished and was a beautiful hotel very much catering to the high-end gay community. We went out by the pool and although cleaned up, this was the same pool where I stood naked some 30 years prior and ended up naked in a National magazine. I went to the "spot" where I thought I had been before and we snapped a few photos to jog the memory.

We had a great time and I came back to Rochester knowing that surgery awaited me. One of our Philly Boyz had an extra ticket to Game #5 in Philadelphia for the 2008 World Series. Maybe out of sympathy for my condition or maybe because he's such a great guy, Jay offered me this ticket.

After flying home to Rochester, I picked up some items from work for a day and a half and proceeded down to Philadelphia to go to the game. The game was Tuesday night. I had all of the pre-op testing scheduled for Thursday. I knew I could easily get down and back in time.

Tuesday's game turned out to be the possible "Close-Out" game. The game that Philadelphia was going to celebrate and go crazy since our last World Series Victory was way back in 1980. All we had to do was WIN THAT GAME. I would be there for the excitement and the city partying that would ensue.

It was a miserably cold and wet night but there was no way they would postpone this game. We dressed accordingly with all the rain-gear and warmth we could muster. The game began in a light, cold rain. As we approached the 4th and then the 5th Inning, the rain got steadier and the night became colder. Add in, that we were all pretty saturated by this point and it made for one miserable but exciting evening. As they approached the bottom of the 5th inning the Fighting Phillies were clinging to a one run lead. The World Series title was only a few innings away.

The rain became too heavy to continue the game and they decided to delay it by pulling out the tarp and hoping that a let up was insight, delaying the game for an hour or so. That hour became two hours. And then that dreaded announcement:

"TONIGHT'S GAME HAS BEEN POSTPONED AND WE WILL ANNOUNCE WHEN IT WILL RESUME ON WEDNESDAY".

This was not great news for me. If they continue the game on Wednesday, I might be able to attend and still get back for all of the hospital crap on Thursday. The problem was that Wednesday's forecast was for more and heavier rain. There was no way they were going to play what may be the final game of the 2008 World Series and pick it up where it left off in terrible weather. It was going to be at least Thursday before the game could continue.

It was not a surprise considering how my luck was running these past few weeks. I was going to have to leave and head back up for the six hour drive to Rochester. I gave my ticket stub to Howard and told him to take one of his kids to what would become the close out game. He did and I had to watch the Phillies clinch the World Series from my living room. At least we won and I was just as happy but to this day I still can't believe that I was there for half of the game when we won the World Series.

Chapter 11
BREAST SURGERY- MASTECTOMY:

The Surgery went smoothly. My largest fear of the sentinel node test came back negative. My cancer was confined and removed. All was looking positive for my recovery. I would just have to keep the drains in for a couple of weeks and begin my regimen of a "PILL A DAY" for the next five years and my life would be back to normal.

Except that was not the case!

Dr. Samuelson referred me to an oncologist for a "routine" follow up. Well, what I thought was going to be routine turned out quite the opposite. He referred me to a "general oncologist" who met with me and informed me that "it wasn't going to be that easy".

My pathology reports stated that although confined and not in the lymph system, it showed a very aggressive form of breast cancer (a high Oncotype score) plus in "his" opinion the pathology report was not conclusive about the cancer being Her2/neu positive. The Her2/neu positive result would mean many more difficulties for me going forward. In his opinion I was going to need chemotherapy.

About the Oncotype DX Breast Cancer Test:

The Oncotype DX breast cancer assay is a test that examines a breast cancer patient's tumor tissue at a molecular level, and gives information about a patient's individual disease. This information can help individualize breast cancer treatment planning and identify options. The Oncotype DX breast cancer test is the only multigene expression test commercially available that has clinical evidence validating its ability to predict the likelihood of chemotherapy benefit as well as recurrence in early-stage breast cancer. The Oncotype DX gene expression assay is intended to be used by women with early-stage (stage I or II), node-negative, estrogen receptor positive (ER+) invasive breast cancer who will be treated with hormone therapy.

 **(Notice that nothing in this paragraph mentions anything to do with MALE breast cancer!)

I was shocked! All of this time I was worried about the sentinel node and the spread of my cancer and none of the time did I ever think that I would need radiation let alone chemotherapy. The thought of going through chemo scared the hell out of me. Everyone knows someone that has been through chemotherapy and knows the side effects and all the unpleasant things it provides. I could not believe that this was happening. The Her2/Nu characteristic was another subject I knew nothing about.

HER2/Nu - According to the Mayo Clinic:

HER2-positive breast cancer is a breast cancer that tests posi-tive for a protein called human epidermal growth factor receptor 2 (HER2), which promotes the growth of cancer cells. In about one of every six breast cancers, the cancer cells make an excess of HER2 due to a gene mutation. This gene mutation and the ele-vated levels of HER2 that it causes can occur in many types of cancer — not only breast cancer. This is a gene mutation that occurs only in the cancer cells and is not a type of mutation that you can inherit from a parent.

HER2-positive breast cancers tend to be more aggressive than other types of breast cancer. They're also less responsive to hormone treatment. However, treatments that specifically target HER2 are very effective. The mostly wide accepted drug is called Herceptin and has shown positive results in treating HER 2/Nu positive breast cancers.

At once I began to search out a different oncologist, preferably one that "specialized" in breast cancer. Recently I was discussing and reliving the episode regarding this "general oncologist" with my current breast oncolo-gist. She explained that in today's cancer world, "NO ONE", should be a "General Oncologist". Cancer is far too complicated of a disease within one type, whether it be breast, prostate, intestinal or brain cancers. Special-ists in these specific cancers still have to deal with 100's if not 1000's of possibilities within their own specialty.

I'm sure that the "General Oncologist" my surgeon referred me to, was doing his best to understand my pathology report, but what he thought was *Her2 Positive* was actually *Her2* indifferent. The initial stain report of the slide was 1.6. *Her2* is positive when it's 3.0 and negative when it's 1.0 or below. My tumor needed additional testing.

A "*Fish Test*" was performed which is a much more in-depth pathology test for the Her2 gene presence. This test came back as *Her2 negative*. That was fortunate, but it wasn't enough to keep me away from chemo all together.

Chapter 12
CHEMO HELL

1**4 Weeks, Four Infusions and about 15 really terrible days!**
Chemotherapy wasn't as bad as I expected. Ok, it wasn't fun, but I expected a lot worse.

I think I was able to stave off many of the ill effects because of the regimen of vitamins and supplements that my brother in law, Gary, had prescribed for me. I wasn't supposed to be taking any of these additional supplements, according to my doctors, but Gary insisted and said, "Just do what I tell you. I'm giving you supplements that will allow you immune system to remain strong and fight off many of the side effects most people get from Chemotherapy".

Usually, the first few days after infusion, I would be fairly fine and normal. When day four or five or six hit, I felt like I just wanted to curl up in a ball and die. I would just lie on my bed and Donna would ask me what she could do to help and I would say nothing. "There's nothing you can do right now and I can't really tell you why I feel so lousy or where it hurts."

One of my worst days was the day President Obama was inaugurated. I was so sick and just sat in bed watching this all day event.

The morphine tablets I was prescribed actually made me feel worse, so I stopped taking them almost immediately after a couple doses.

After each treatment the sickness lasted slightly longer. Buy the fourth treatment, I was sick for almost five days.

One of the most surprising issues I experienced was after my second infusion I received a call that evening from my oncologist.

At first I was surprised that she was calling me at all, since I didn't hear from her following my first treatment. She asked me how I was doing and how I felt and I explained that I felt like crap after being infused with poison all day. Then, she proceeded to say, "Well, I'm calling to tell you that you received a drug today that you weren't supposed to get".

"WHAT", I responded? "What exactly are you talking about?" Dr. Miller continued, "You see after treatment number two, for all of my "FEMALE" post-menopausal patients, we give an additional medication called Boniva". Boniva is on the market to assist with Osteoporosis or bone brittleness. "We give it to our breast cancer patients because chemo can sometimes accelerate the bone issues. I wrote the order, but I didn't intend for you to get it", she explained. To this day, I haven't figured out what "I wrote the order but didn't intend for you to have it" exactly meant?

Ok, so now what? She went on to tell me that there probably wouldn't be any side effects and that with "only one treatment" really nothing was going to happen. I guess I was relieved that I wasn't going to grow a vagina, but I was still totally frustrated by this conversation.

Basically, another indication of "A Man with A Women's Disease"! They give this drug during treatment number two to all of their breast cancer patients. And 99% of their breast cancer patients are female, so just in orderly fashion she wrote the order and they administered the drug. They never stopped to think or figure that this was a guy and he couldn't be post-menopausal? Nope, just follow the normal procedures. It was just another product of our physicians being taxed with too many patients and not enough hours in the day. Another indication that you have to be totally aware of every procedure, drug or process you are going through.

I actually questioned the drug when the infusion nurse brought it to my attention. I insisted that I had just left my oncologist, which is normal procedure before getting infused to check all of your blood levels and labs. I stated that she never mentioned another drug. I actually had the nurse call down to my oncology office and "double-check" that I was in fact supposed to receive this additional drug infused. After about 45 minutes the nurse came back and said, "Yes, I spoke with Dr. Miller's nurse and she confirmed you are to have this additional drug." Ok, I checked and they checked so Donna and I said "ok".

Choosing the type of chemotherapy treatment proved to be one of the hardest parts of the whole process. During my first visits to the surgeon and early on I was assured that once surgery was completed, all I would have to do was take some pill once a day for five years and I'd be all set!

The pills were Tamoxifen, which as it turned out was one of two alternatives for the five year regimen. The other was a fairly new drug on the market called Arimidex. Basically one stops you from producing the hormones that breast cancer lives on. The other, stops or tricks the cells into thinking they don't need any more hormones and the cancer cells starve and die off. This choice was the second of my two heart to heart discussions with my now attending oncologist, Dr. Fran Miller. (Just recently, many studies have been showing that the Tamoxifen five year regimen, may be better served if the patient stayed on the medication for 10 years)

Dr. Miller is one of the leading breast oncologists in the Comprehensive Breast Center at Strong Memorial Hospital/ Wilmot Cancer Center on the University of Rochester Campus. Dr. Miller is a fairly stoic doctor as I found out when I first met her. She prescribes to most of what the Memorial Sloan Kettering Cancer Center in New York City states. I soon discovered that every oncologist has her/ his own methods for treatment and that most times their decisions are shaped by some major institution and what the institution and their studies consistently finds and directs.

Another of these decision maker institutions happens to be Dana Farber Cancer Hospital in Boston or MD Anderson Cancer Centers based in Texas. A third example would be those who religiously follow the protocols put forth by the San Antonio Breast Cancer Symposium. A gathering of 100's of the brightest minds in the breast cancer field coming together to compare notes and studies. This usually occurs in October or November once a year.

In between my surgery and before I was to begin any follow up chemo treatment, I continued to work doing my job as National Accounts Director and overseeing the East coast sales team for my uniform company.

I was in Boston on business about a week before Christmas 2008. As my luck would have it, Boston was about to experience one of its worst blizzards in 30 years. After getting to the airport on a Friday morning and waiting for three hours to leave Boston, I was informed that my flight was cancelled. I immediately called my Hilton diamond hot line to find me a room which they aptly accommodated.

After checking into my room which was a couple of blocks from the large Copley Square Mall in downtown Boston, I decided to brave the weather and hike over to the mall to get something to eat and possibly do a little shopping. After all I was stuck in Boston, snowed in on this Friday and I wasn't getting home at any point on this day.

The weather was getting bad. Really, really bad! I somehow made it to the mall, (wondering how the hell I was going to get back), but none the less I was there and it was dry and most of the people were leaving to head home to the Boston suburbs.

I decided to go into the Legal Sea Foods and sit at the bar for some food. I was sitting on the last seat of the bar before it turned to provide three additional adjacent seats. I ordered my lunch of a crab cake sand-wich and some "Chowda" (speaking Bostonian). Before my food arrived this woman wanders into the restaurant, sits on the side rail adjacent to me and she has two briefcases and lots of papers with her. The bartender approaches her and says, "WHAT ARE YOU DOING HERE, IN THE MIDDLE OF THE DAY"?

Ok, so I've always been a bit of an eves-dropper. My wife always yells at me for listening and being interested in other people's conversations. And now I'm totally bored, knowing I have at least a day to kill in Boston in this blizzard, so I need some form of entertainment to keep my interest.

The woman responds: "They closed my clinic!" She continued, "I have all of these patients who need treatment and they fucking closed my clinic." The bartender responded, "Because of the weather?" "Yes, and it's not that bad out" she states with an angry scowl. The bartender says, "I'll get you your usual". Her usual was some special wine that he extracted from a bot-tom cabinet.

I'm sitting there with my "*chowda*" and now I'm really interested. What type of clinic I'm thinking? Do I engage her in conversation at this point? Do I wait for her to get through her first glass of wine before I begin to talk? I'm curious, lonely and need a friend. The place was mostly empty by this point.

Of course if you know me, I couldn't resist and I lean toward her and say, "Excuse me, but I couldn't help overhearing you. What type of clinic do you work for?" At first she had no interest in me or talking about her work, but finally relented and said that she works for Dana Farber and that the clinic they closed because of the snow was the treatment infusion center. We conversed a little more when I asked her, "what type of doctor are you and what do you treat"?

She then stated, "I'm an OB-GYN oncologist but I specialize in BREAST CANCER!"

WOW!!

Here I am sitting in a snow storm in some random restaurant bar and there are very few people left in the restaurant or even the mall and the person next to me is a "Breast Cancer Specialist"! What are the odds?

People talk about fate and crap like that all the time, but some force of nature must have known that I was at a crossroads for treatment and needed some information and put this woman right next to me. Not only with a chance to converse, but with neither of us having any place to be or go at this point in time.

Of course my next statement to her was "wow, that's incredible, because I'm a Breast Cancer patient!"

Fortunately, because I was a male, she was as much interested in me and my journey as I was in her opinions. She began talking about recently returning from the San Antonio Breast Cancer Symposium where she learned a lot of new information. She actually gave me the URL to San Antonio's website and told me how to access the information from all the studies published on their site.

She then asked me what I was going to do this night while I'm stranded in Boston and where I was staying. I told her and she said that about two blocks down and one block over from my hotel, there was a 12-plex movie theatre and that I should go see this new movie that just opened. She had just seen it and it was one of the best movies she's ever seen. "Slum Dog Millionaire".

Ok I thought, but I've never heard of it? And when she gave me the story-line, I thought "ehh" that's not my kind of movie, but I'll think about it.

Before we both departed the restaurant and after her third glass of that special wine that only the bartender knew about, she made sure to write down on a cocktail napkin for me, the regimen of chemo she thought would most likely benefit me. I saved that napkin in my Boston trip file, not knowing how important it would become to me about two months later.

I did fight my way through the snow storm, for those three very long, very wet and very cold blocks and found that 12-Plex of theatres. I got up to the window and looked at all the large billboards for all the movies playing that night and I just couldn't see myself choosing this "Slum Dog" movie? I kept thinking I'd go see something else. But some force of nature kept saying to me that this chance meeting with this doctor was so circumstance and she was so high on this flick, how could I tempt fate and not see it?

Well the movie as you probably know by now, was very, very good and went on to win all kinds of Academy Awards, so the good doctor knew of what she spoke!

About a month later and after the holidays I had to go out to my office in San Diego for some meetings. I live in Rochester, NY, but I work for a California based company, so about three or four times per year I travel cross country. Our office is in a suburb of San Diego, so usually it's not that tough of trip to make, at least weather wise, especially in the middle of winter.

One of my closest friends at our company is a guy named Jeff who at the time basically did the same job as I was doing except on the West Coast. Even before I joined them when I had my own distribution company in this industry that sold many of their products, Jeff and I became friends. Jeff is a tall slender South African gentleman. Our company is a family business started by three brothers whose father was a uniform clothing manufacturer in South Africa and they came to the U.S. to start their own company, specializing in the culinary uniform business.

When I went out to the office, Jeff would always invite me to his house for a meal or even to stay with him and his wife Sandi.

Over the years Sandi and I became very friendly. Unlike Jeff, she was a New Yorker who moved to the west coast. A virtual sweetheart of a person who could never do enough for you. Sandi was a pretty high roller in the world of San Diego residential real estate and their home showed it!

Sandi was also a breast cancer survivor! And not your ordinary survivor as she had metastasized breast cancer for over 20 years! On this trip out and with my recent diagnosis, Sandi called me to talk and she wanted me to go see her oncologist who she referred to, as her "God"! Dr. John Link. I didn't realize it then but Dr. John Link is regarded as one of the world's foremost experts on breast cancer. His book, "The Breast Cancer Survival Guide" is sold at almost every supermarket's checkout counter and book store. He is not the kind of doctor you get an appointment with easily, especially as a second or third opinion.

Dr. Link is based just outside of Los Angeles. Sandi made the contact arrangements for me and I set up an appointment on my way out to San Diego, flying into Los Angeles and then driving down to San Diego. I was hopeful that Dr. Link would be the one to tell me that I didn't need chemo treatments and that I was good to go. No such luck. But after a thorough 90 minute visit, I left Dr. Link's office with some basic instructions and one critical piece of paper.

Dr. Link had told me that I did need to have Chemo and "whatever I do chemotherapy wise, do not have one drug included". As a matter of fact he drew out a diagram with "A, C, T" on it and circled the "A" and then put a Big "X" Through the "A". The "A" stood for Adriamycin, which is a standard in the chemo drug world in treating breast cancer and many additional cancers as well. Dr. Link informed me that he had about three to five women who he cured of breast cancer, but contracted blood disorders. In his opinion, Adriamycin was the culprit, although he had no exact proof.

He stated that the recent San Antonio Breast Cancer Symposium had study after study that showed that A, C, T was no more effective and offered no more lower recurrence numbers or survival rate extensions than "C & T" alone. Cytoxan and Taxotere.

I left Dr. Link's office and drove down to San Diego, stopping to have dinner in Newport Beach with some friends, totally depressed that Dr. Link concurred that I needed to have some sort of chemotherapy. My head and emotions were spinning out of control. I can't even remember actually driving the next hour plus. It was almost like my rental car was on auto-pilot.

Dr. Miller had also told me this fact as well as the by chance specialist I met in Boston in December. Three out of three oncologists thought I needed some form of chemotherapy and that basically meant I was going to be pretty sick for while!

I can't remember much of that dinner with my friends and it was with two people that I truly enjoy, Diane and Dave Weinstein. I only mention them by name here because our friendship is truly an amazing story.

Chapter 13
A REUNION AFTER 40 YEARS IN BUENOS AIRES:

In 2006 my sons Matthew and Jameson were recruited by a good friend who was high up in the USA Maccabi organization. Maccabi is the International Federation of Jewish Athletes. Every four years, Maccabi brings in Jewish athletes from over 35 countries to Israel to compete in an Olympic style competition. My son Matthew was an outstanding natural athlete and was a three sport varsity standout in high school in football, baseball and basketball. Ok, maybe he didn't stand out as much in basketball, but he was a good player, just a little size restricted at 5' 9" tall. Jameson, by contrast played all sports until he decided he was going to be dedicated to basketball full time. A little taller than Matt but with the sweetest left handed "jump shot" a high school kid could have. Jameson had a great "handle" along with being left handed, made him very difficult to cover.

Craig had been after Matt while he was in college playing baseball for RIT (Rochester Institute of Technology) to join Maccabi and become an "OPEN" fast-pitch softball player. Matt was always hesitant for two reasons: First, he wasn't Jewish. I am, but my wife Donna is not. She is Italian, Roman Catholic. Under Jewish law, the child bores the religion of the mother. "From the womb". Secondly, while still playing baseball in college, Matt wasn't about to "mess up his swing" by switching to fast-pitch softball. He also didn't have any interest in going to Israel. My wife was always (and still is) afraid of going there, thinking that we would go to Israel and immediately a bomb would go off.

In 2006 Matt had already graduated from college as a packaging engineer and was a member of the working world. The interesting thing about Maccabi is that they compete in Israel every four years, but in the middle two years, they have what is known as the Pan Am games, which is basically the same thing on a smaller scale, with mostly countries from the western hemisphere sending athletes.

Craig came calling again and convinced me, Donna and Matt that this would be a good trial for Matt to go with the delegation to Buenos Aires, Argentina and see how he could compete and if he would even like the whole experience. They do accentuate the Jewish part. Matt was eligible because under Maccabi rules, you only need one parent to be Jewish to qualify. I then asked about Jameson who was just finishing up college as Journalism major and still had some good basketball in him, even though he hadn't played since high school. Craig said that he knew Matt was good enough and would have to transition his game to fast pitch, but that Jameson would have to try out. Jameson went back into the gym, got himself in shape and made the Open Basketball team that was headed to Argentina. We would go as a family, although the athletes traveled separately with their respective teams.

Because of the amount of Jews all traveling and exposed together, Maccabi is very, very careful to take all precautions with their athletes and guests. Most people are aware that "groups of Jews" can be targets anywhere in the world. We always traveled in groups to and from every venue and the athletes had "machine gun- armed guards" on their buses. We had just finished up the first day of competition and we were ushered to a waiting area for the buses to arrive that would bring all the guests of the athletes to the opening ceremony venue.

While waiting in this collection area (where we were safe) my friend Craig comes up to me and says, "hey, come over here, I want you to meet a guy who grew up in your neighborhood back in Philly". He drags me over and before he can say anything to either of us, this guy looks at me and says, "HARVEY"? "Harvey Singer who had his house burn down on Fanshawe Street?" I immediately knew who he was, it was Dave Weinstein.

Dave and I were best friends through elementary school and some of Junior High. We lived in row houses in Northeast Philadelphia, which had these long driveways going down the backs of the homes separating the two streets. In this case Fanshawe which I lived on and Unruh where Dave lived. The backs of our house and garages were virtually right across the driveway from each other. We spent countless hours playing basket-ball using the "wires" that ran up the entire length of the street. Once in a while, we took out a garage window which was directly beneath those wires. The wires were about nine feet above the ground and perfectly fit a regulation basketball with a little delay to show you scored.

Dave and I walked to elementary school every day together and his first "girlfriend" was my cousin Cindy who lived right across from me on Fanshawe Street. To this day, he is still infatuated with Cousin Cindy. His wife knows all about it and she just goes along with the flow when Dave brings her up. He is also very fond of a girl named "Helene" who we went to elementary school with. Helene was the biggest and most mature of all the 5th grade girls and "developed" far earlier than all of the other girls. She knew this and used to take all the boys over to her house and give us "private bathroom viewings" of her very developed breasts. That was one of the first things Dave reminded me of after this by chance meeting at this bus stop, after Cindy, of course. I guess he never got over that first breast sighting.

Dave was one of the first people to watch as our house on Fanshawe Street burned down. It was a gas heater explosion and fortunately, we all got out ok, but my parents lost everything. We moved to a temporary apart-ment until my parents found a new house they could afford and where they wanted to be. The fire was in October and I completed the school year, from a temporary housing location. At the end of that school year, Dave's family up and moved away to California. That was 1968. I never knew where he went and never heard from him again... UNTIL WAITING FOR THIS BUS in Buenos Aries, Argentina, 41 years later!

Talk about weird. Dave and I began to recount our lives from 41 years ago and all that had transpired since. He was now a pretty well- to -do attorney in Newport Beach, CA and had a sweetheart of a wife named Diane. They were there in Argentina because their two kids a boy and a girl were competing in volley ball. We ended up riding the bus together, playing catch up and sat together through the opening ceremonies, which was an Olympic style spectacular. We spent much of that week having din-ners together and it was like 41 years meant nothing. We were good friends again.

So while I was heading down to San Diego, it all seemed like a perfect time to get to see Dave and Diane again. I had not seen them since Argentina, although we had kept in touch on a regular basis. I remember nothing about that dinner except that Dave, who is a vegetarian, actually tried to eat a piece of fish. I remember it not going down so well. Otherwise, they knew I had a lot of shit going on and that my head was spinning. They were very supportive and I left early and headed down to my hotel.

The next day was a work day in the office. I put a call in early to Dr. Miller back in Rochester wanting to discuss with her what I had learned from Dr. Link. Before she had a chance to call me back, my CEO called me into his office to "catch up".

He and I had a nice conversation when he said to me, "You know we've really been thinking that you've done such a good job on the East Coast and that maybe you would consider moving out here to San Diego to run all of sales"?

Of course Martin had no idea what I had going on at this point. He knew that I had breast cancer surgery and also assumed (like I did) that it was all behind me. He caught me off guard, because I never expected these words to come out of his mouth and right now I had much bigger issues in my life going on. The last thing I needed was to pick up my life and move back to the west coast and take on all of this responsibility and challenges. Maybe if I were 15 years younger and had perfect health I may have considered this offer? But right now, I had far too much on my plate. Add in the fact that our company was "TIPPING" and the office was so busy it was almost toxic in nature to be there, I flatly turned him down. I then began to fill Martin in on what was happening with my health and the fact that I was facing three months plus of chemotherapy.

As I departed his office my phone rang and it was Dr. Miller. We began to talk about my second opinion visit and the fact that the A C T regimen that she wanted me to have, was being questioned by another specialist and by me personally. I remember her saying to me "You have a very aggressive form of breast cancer. Don't you want the best possible and strongest drugs we have to beat this disease?"

"Ummm, not if it's going to give me Leukemia", I thought.

We agreed to meet to discuss the chemo-topic upon my return. In the interim Dr. Miller stated that she would take my case and present it to her "Tumor Board". This Tumor Board is a group of oncologists from University of Rochester Medical Center that meets twice a month and discusses all the most difficult and complicated cases.

When I returned home I had my scheduled appointment with Dr. Miller.

Donna went with me to the "Comprehensive Breast Cancer Center" at Strong Hospital. We checked in and the receptionist gave me the obligatory paperwork to fill out. The paper work asked questions of normalcy like what medications I had been utilizing. How much alcohol had I been consuming? Any new pains, mental anguish or trouble sleeping? All of these were pretty basic questions.

And then I came across a question that I couldn't believe I had to answer. I looked at Donna and said, ***"DO I HAVE VAGINAL DRYNESS?"*** We both just started laughing finding overwhelming humor with the question. I said to Donna, "I guess you'll have to answer this one". **A Man with a Woman's Disease**, once again.

I finally get called back and have the regulatory weigh in and blood pressure tests before entering an exam room where Dr. Miller "will be with you shortly". Dr. Miller comes in and then proceeds to tell me that she presented my case to her Tumor Board and that 50% of the doctors agreed with me and the other 50% agreed with her, so she would leave the decision up to me.

GREAT! I now get to decide, without any really specific medical knowledge or training, on which chemotherapy regimen I am going to have. How would I possibly answer this question? It could possibly mean life or death to me. Do I go with my attending doctor or do I trust this guy I've met once on the west coast, but who my friend Sandi refers to, as her God?

And then I remembered the NAPKIN!

That by chance snowstorm meeting at the bar at the Legal Sea Foods in Boston and the oncologist that just happened to write down on that small white cocktail napkin what treatment she felt was best for me. Now where did I put that napkin?

Whenever I travel for business or pleasure I keep a file with all the information on flights, hotels, receipts for my expense accounts etc. I went home and scoured through my past files and I find the file from that Boston trip. I begin to rummage through the file and low and behold, there it was! A little crumpled up but still it was perfectly legible.

Cytoxan/ Taxotere. NO "A"!

Now it's not that I don't trust my attending oncologist, in fact I think she's brilliant. But I'm following my friend "Sandi's God" and my "everything happens for a reason" fate meeting in Boston and I'm going with it! It's my choice and I'll have to live…. Or Die… with the outcome.

Chapter 14
I AM SANDI

Consider this a weird coincidence, but as I pen this very important chapter in my journey, I do so because hurricane SANDY has knocked out my internet. I cannot get on the company server to work, but we do have full power here at home.

"Sandy", the hurricane has just completed knocking out half of the Northeast U.S. All of the airports in NY and NJ are closed. Atlantic City, my youth summer home and an island where many friends and family have their summer homes is completely flooded out. The New York Subway and MTA (buses) are all shut down. My eldest son who was supposed to move from one Hoboken apartment to another the next day is trapped in New Brunswick, after being evacuated.

The following weekend I would travel most of the way and my son Matt would meet me as Donna and I were going to assist by taking "Cassius" (his dog) off his hands and until he figured out where he was going to live. By the time Matt got re settled with a new roommate we were still taking care of his dog. Additionally about this time, Matt was being recruited by a large California company. He decided to take the position and move back to the Los Angeles area of California.

Donna and I hadn't had a dog since our beloved Chesapeake Bay retriever, Corby, passed away. I was constantly begging her to get another dog but she sighted how tough our schedules were at this point in our lives with me traveling for business and with her usually working some 60+ hours per week in her business. In this case, we didn't really have a choice as "Cash" was our Grand-Dog! You can't turn your back on family, especially not your son and Grand-Doggie.

We have easily adapted and we are both in love with Cassius. Cash is a rescue Pit-Bull mix and I can still remember our response when our boys told us they were going to adopt a Pit-Bull! "Are you guys out of your mind"?

Well once we researched the breed. and we found that Pit Bulls are actually passive loving animals, and it's very unfortunate that people train them to fight and treat them to a life of abuse. Cash is actually part Pit and part Boxer and is a beautiful brindle color. He's an amazing animal who can only love and love you some more. He doesn't have a mean bone in his body and will play with any other dog or any person who offers time to him. He has made our house a home again since both boys moved out several years ago. It's such a shame that that the media perpetuates such inaccuracies about the Pit Bull breed. You never hear of a Labrador or a Poodle biting someone, even though I'm fairly certain it happens every day. But as soon as an abused Pit Bull bites someone, it becomes front page news.

Cash and his five siblings were born and just tossed on the side of a road. Rescue-a-Bull is a great organization that offers these wonderful, loving animals a chance at a permanent home. My boys were smarter than their parents and did their homework and rescued one of the most loving animals I've ever been around.

Cassius in front of the Fireplace in our home

Hurricane Sandy has cause billions of dollars in damage. That was the "Bad Sandy". This is the "Good, actually Great, SANDI"!

Sandi Lewis, the wife of my closest work confidant Jeffrey Abelsohn was a rock of a woman! Sandi was diagnosed with breast cancer six months after her only child, a daughter, Sarah was born. Jeff had two other children from a previous marriage, but Sarah was Sandi and Jeff's only child together.

Sandi was a New Yorker, transposed to become a very important realtor in the San Diego residential real estate market. Most New Yorker's have a unique advantage when they transition to the west coast, especially California, for business acumen. No one conducts business like those who were trained in New York. I'm not sure what the reasons or rationale is for it, but it just is! Maybe it's the pace of business. I always said to my bosses, "New Yorkers want to order it today and get it yesterday"! Plus New Yorker's are relentless when it comes to quality and price.

Of course the hierarchy of my company being of South African descent, they never quite understood the concept. Fortunately Jeff, also a South African was much more like a New Yorker than a laid back South African or Southern Californian in his personality. Maybe that's why Sandi and Jeff were able to hook up? Her cancer made their relationship much more tumultuous than it needed to be. Cancer will do that to you.

Shortly after diagnosis, Sandi had a full bi-lateral mastectomy (both breasts removed) and subsequent reconstruction. Unfortunately, her cancer had spread to the lymph nodes and many rounds of chemo were to follow.

I had met Sandi several times before my cancer was first diagnosed. She was always open and welcoming to me in their home and treated me like family. I think to Sandi, I was sort of family being from back east and she knew how close Jeff and I had become.

After my diagnosis, during the time post-surgery and before chemo, while I was out in California at our office I went over to Jeff and Sandi's home to discuss my options. She had already set up my "second opinion" with Dr. Link and she was very concerned for me. Sandi was also BRCA 2.

To this day I can hear her still saying to me, "I've beaten this thing for almost 20 years, and you will have no issues beating it"! Sandi kept pounding it into me, "I can … You Will! I can…You Will!"

When Jeff wasn't around or within hearing distance, Sandi would confide in me that most importantly to her, she just wanted to see Sarah graduate high school! She would constantly tell me that. Sarah was about 15 at the time. Sarah was a true "Valley Girl… for Sure". I remember going with Sarah and her friends with Sandi in her car to take the girls to the mall. The conversation in the back seat was absolutely priceless. Just imagine "Four Valley Girls" talking about their upcoming adventure to the mall.

Sandi had multiple recurrences of her breast cancer with small tumors in her neck and on her clavicle bone. She was constantly going for PET Scans and all the other myriad of tests that recurrent cancer patients consume. Inevitably, those tests lead to more chemo.

Finally a breakthrough occurred.

While Jeff was working a trade show he had heard there was a conference going on in the same hotel which involved a new type of treatment for BRCA patients. It was called a Parp Inhibitor and there were three different clinical trials going on with three different drug companies. As is Jeff's nature, he wouldn't be stopped. He basically broke into these meetings and tracked down one of the lead doctors from Los Angeles to plead his case and to get Sandi into the trial. No easy task. They had mountains of restrictions as to who could be considered.

You have to understand the drug companies that do these clinical trial tests are looking for the best possible results in terms of numbers. They want to give themselves the best possible chance of being first on the market to launch this new drug.

For example, Viagra was well ahead of the curve in creation of a drug to cure Erectile Dysfunction. Other drug companies created Cialis and Levitra later on and had to play catch up for market share. Fortunately even though Viagra leads by a wide margin, there is such a big market for E.D. drugs, they're all doing very well, financially speaking.

PARP Inhibitors for BRCA don't possess that same large market that E.D. Drugs do. Astra Zeneca was leading the way and Jeff was going to find a way to get Sandi into the clinical trial. Sandi and Jeff knew it was probably her last and only chance to survive this disease.

PARP inhibitors work in a mysterious way, by basically "repairing the gene mutation" and in doing so, actually causes active disease to shrink and eventually go away. Their testing showed almost a 70% positive test result and these numbers were rising.

Jeff and Sandi were relentless and got through to the lead doctor who eventually got Sandi in for Pre-Testing. She needed to have undergone at least three rounds of chemo in the past. She needed to have active tumors in her body and a variety of other circumstances before they would accept her into the trial. After months of back and forth testing, Sandi was admitted to the program. Finally, a possible cure for her breast cancer. I can still recall how elated they were when they told me she was going to begin the trial and how much hope they both had. Sandi had gone from hoping to see her daughter graduate from high school to hoping to see her graduate from college.

The elation was short lived. Sandi was being "excused" from the trial approximately six weeks after she began because the doctors running the trial for the drug company felt like they couldn't help her and it wouldn't work. As stated earlier, they want "Positive" results. Sandi was devastated! She basically knew that this was her last chance for a cure and that it would be all down hill from this point forward.

IT WAS!

Some two plus years later and after more chemo and more natural therapies of all types including Vitamin C infusions on a weekly basis, Sandi's condition was deteriorating. In late August 2011, I was out in California for an office visit. It was a Friday evening and I was invited over to Jeff and Sandi's to have a Shabbos Dinner. I remember going into the house and Sandi was captive in her bedroom. I sat on the side of her bed and we talked. We spoke nothing about her cancer or the fact that it had spread to her brain. Nope, just about life in general. She was always asking me "how I was doing". That was the type of person Sandi was. She was always concerned for the other person.

Somehow she would make it out of bed in time for dinner with some other of her closest friends. We lit the Shabbos candles and we had a very nice meal that her friends cooked up right in her wonderful kitchen of their amazing home. Shortly after the meal, Sandi basically said she needed to go back to bed. Of course we all obliged. A couple of hours passed and it was time to leave and I asked Jeff if I could see her before leaving. Jeff said wait a minute and went into the bedroom of their sprawling ranch house which sits up on a ravine in the San Diego hills. He emerged and said to me, "Sandi says to tell you goodbye".

I will never forget that moment because I knew at the time it was very unlikely that I would ever see her again. I left and drove back to my hotel and all I could think about was Sandi.

She had been through so much. She fought so hard. She tried everything possible to beat this disease. Sarah was now a college freshman at the University of Arizona. She and her mother were extremely close and as she got older, she became more realistic about her mother's outcome. She would sit and talk with her in bed or just read her the paper. It didn't matter. They needed each other. Sandi's condition deteriorated throughout the fall. Every week it seemed like they would give her a week or so to live. Sandi was so fucking tough, she refused to give in. She refused to die.

By early December Jeff was forced to make the decision to bring in home hospice. Hospice said "a couple of days". This became a couple of weeks. Sandi was not going to go easily and always defied everyone's predictions or odds. She had done so her entire life and as it was coming to a close, Sandi continued to prove that she was going to be "too tough to die".

I received a call at about 4:00 PM on Saturday just before Christmas 2011. Sandi was gone and the funeral was going to be the next day. I was back in Schenectady at my mother in law's house celebrating Christmas with the family. I had no way to get out to San Diego in less than 24 hours on a Christmas weekend. To this day it still bothers me that I didn't get to go and say goodbye. Jeff of course understood but that was his way. Here today, buried tomorrow. It's the way the old Jewish tradition works and my South African brothers are very old school when it comes to Jewish custom.

I named this chapter "I Am Sandi" because that was Sandi Lewis' email address. I will never forget what she did and how she cared about me. I will never forget her demeanor and power of positive thinking. She was truly a friend to many and much more to me. I can only hope that she rests in peace and no longer has the pain that afflicted her through her 20 year battle.

On another note, even though Sandi always thought she knew this, Sarah has been subsequently tested for the BRCA2 gene mutation. Sandi always believed that she had passed the gene along and prayed that she didn't. When Jeff called me to tell me the results of Sarah's BRCA test, I knew as soon as I heard his voice that Sarah was positive.

She was.

I said to Jeff; "it's a good thing that Sandi didn't know that before she passed". To which Jeff immediately responded…

"Oh, She Knew"!

Sandi Lewis Abelsohn knew it all and lived her life knowing her outcome. I miss her dearly, and I'm sure 100's of others do as well.

Sandi with her daughter Sarah 2011

Chapter 15
PROSTATE CANCER:

About 18 months, prior to my breast cancer diagnosis, I was having an issue with a rising PSA. I had some of the symptoms of an enlarged prostate and I was (supposedly) under the watch from a notable Rochester, NY urologist. This doctor came highly recommended from a friend who is a registered nurse and her husband, a successful doctor in the area, who also battled prostate cancer.

For any man over 40, the "routine" annual physical and the joy of that rubber gloved covered finger penetrating that "O 'so' Sacred Area" followed up by the PSA blood test, is something we all look forward to every year.

I never understood how anyone would want this job! Can you imagine what some guy's butt holes look like? Then to take all that schooling and years upon years of residency etc. to become an urologist is hard to fathom.

A few years later I was hospitalized for something called a lymphocele and I was under the care of the lead urologist at Strong Memorial Hospital. He traveled for his rounds with a harem of young, pretty resident urologists. I remember asking one of them why she, with all the options in medicine today, would choose to be a urologist? Her response was very interesting. First she said that most urologic patients tend to be older gentlemen and she really liked working with those guys who were always so nice to her. (Yes, probably because she was young and pretty). Her other reason was that urology is one of the hardest specialties to get into. Only the smartest and best doctors get into the club. To be accepted means you've made it and you're smarter or a better doctor than the rest.

Well not this guy who was treating me. I'll leave his name out, although to this day I blame him for where I am today, urologically speaking!

I would go every two months to see this urologist. My PSA continued to rise from five to six from seven to nine. Finally he decided that even though his "digital test" (the lovely finger up the ass to feel the prostate) showed him no signs that I should have prostate cancer, he would do a prostate biopsy on me anyway.

First let me clarify all of the myths about prostate biopsies. They do not have to go down through your penis to accomplish this. Now with that stated and now that your legs have stopped quivering, I can tell you it's not much fun the other way either. The way they do prostate biopsies is to use a needle gun which they shoot into your butt, ultra-sound guided and they take, by shooting this gun and removing sections or pieces of your prostate, about 10-12 samples of tissue from your prostate. They do attempt to "numb" the area of the rectal wall with a little Novocain type drug which doesn't help all that much.

In my case back in 2007, the caring doctor (who had the personality of a door knob), took nine samples and sent them off to the lab. A few days later he called and told me all the slides were negative! YES! A great day it was…. Or so I thought.

I remained under this urologist's care all through my breast cancer ordeal. He knew my sister was BRCA 2. He knew my family history. He also knew that BRCA in males is usually over 70% likely to cause prostate cancer. He treated me symptomatically for the abnormal stream of my urine and the fact that I had the urge to "go" frequently and often. When you don't have prostate cancer and you do have symptoms, they call it BPH. The "B" stands for benign. Many men 55+ have these issues.

ACCORDING TO THE MAYO CLINIC:

Prostate gland enlargement is a common condition as men get older. Also called benign prostatic hyperplasia (BPH) and prostatic hypertrophy, prostate gland enlargement can cause bothersome urinary symptoms. Untreated prostate gland enlargement can block the flow of urine out of the bladder and can cause bladder, urinary tract or kidney problems.

There are several effective treatments for prostate gland enlargement. In deciding the best option for you, you and your doctor will consider your particular symptoms, the size of your prostate, other health problems you may have and your preferences. Your choices may also depend on what treatments are available in your area. Treatments for prostate gland enlargement include medications, lifestyle changes and surgery.

The PSA test has received its share of controversy lately and many feel that a higher PSA is not always a sign of prostate cancer. They feel there are too many biopsies being done needlessly and that they produce too many false positives. Yes, the test is not fun. Yes you urinate and ejaculate blood for weeks after the biopsies. That's always a pleasant sight to your wife. But you have to weigh out the positives of finding prostate cancer early which is almost 99% curable while it is still encapsulated, with the negative, which is missing it and having the cancer spread to the lymph nodes or the bones. Prostate cancer LOVES to metastasize to the bones!

But mine was NEGATIVE! It was a great day when he called to tell me the results. I remember how relieved I was that I wouldn't have to go through prostate surgery and that I didn't have cancer!

Eighteen months later I was diagnosed with breast cancer. No longer was prostate cancer front and center of my mind and I felt comfortable being watched every three months by this top rated physician. I had bigger fish to fry in my life now and it was dealing with my breast cancer.

Over those three years my PSA continued to rise and Dr. "know it all" kept assuring me that I had nothing to worry about. A high PSA does not mean prostate cancer and he had already done a biopsy, he continually expressed to me.

Finally when my PSA reached over 13 and a year and half after all of my breast cancer ordeals, we decided to do another biopsy. "JUST TO BE SURE" as the doctor put it.

The whole time and even while he was performing this lovely test in his office, he was assuring me that there's no way this was going to be positive. He kept saying, "I've never felt a bump, a lump or any hardness in your prostate". Since they use ultrasound for placement he said, "There's nothing here in the ultrasound that even begins to worry me about your possibility of having prostate cancer". I left the office trusting and feeling pretty confident that we were just going through the motions and just to be certain. The doctor said, "I'll call you in four or five days with the results".

Two days later, while I'm driving in my blue tooth activated car, my phone rings. I hit the speaker button as the number came in as "restricted". "Hi Harvey, its Doctor" (Nameless). " I can't believe I have to tell you this, but you have prostate cancer"! Silence on my end, as I tried to rationalize what he assured me just 48 hours earlier would not happen. "Believe me I'm just as shocked as you are!"

"Wanna Bet?" (I was thinking)

"I never in all my years of practice thought this would come back positive. I'm sorry but you need to see me in the office this week so we can decide how to attack your problem".

Eighteen months post breast surgery, chemo, and follow up meds, I now have to deal with another cancer.

Although the BRCA2 very likely caused both cancers, they were not related or metastasized from one another but actually two separate cancers.

Once again my mind started to race 1000 miles per hour. Now What?

I did go with my wife to meet with the doctor. We wanted to hear what he had to say and recommend. But the entire time, I had no intentions of having this doctor or any of his associates treat or operate on me. He detailed to me that biopsy showed a higher "Gleason Score".

All Prostate Cancers are rated by this scale some guy named Dr. Gleason created to "rate" the growth and possible spread of the cancer in the prostate. Using my age, my family history and my Gleason score, he determined that surgery was my only course of action.

According to Johns Hopkins University Medicine:

Prostate Cancer on Needle Biopsy

When your prostate was biopsied, the samples taken were studied under the microscope by a specialized doctor with many years of training called a pathologist. The pathology report tells your treating doctor the diagnosis in each of the samples to help manage your care. This FAQ sheet is designed to help you understand the medical language used in the pathology report.

1. *What is "adenocarcinoma of the prostate"?*

   Adenocarcinoma of the prostate is a type of cancer (tumor) with a wide range of behavior from cases which are very slow growing with a low risk of causing men harm to cases which are more aggressive.

2. *What is a "core"?*

   The urologist samples the prostate by removing thin threads of tissue with a hollow needle, each one referred to as a "core", from different areas of the prostate. The number of cores which contain cancer, as well as the amount of cancer present on each core, has a relationship to the tumorâ€™s prognosis.

3. *What is the "Gleason grade" or "Gleason score"?*

   The Gleason score is a measurement of how aggressive your tumor is likely to be. It is made by a pathologist looking at the cancer under the microscope.

4. *What are the numbers in the Gleason score, for example 3+4=7 or 3+3=6?*

   Prostate cancer can have several patterns under the microscope, which are each assigned a different number. The first number in the score is the most common and the second number in the score is the next most common pattern seen under the microscope. The individual patterns typically range 3 to 5 on biopsy, with 3 being least aggressive and 5 the most aggressive. They are added together to get your total "Gleason grade" or "Gleason score", which typically ranges from 6 to 10. For example, in a Gleason score 3+4=7, most of the tumor is pattern 3 and less is pattern 4 and they are added together for a Gleason score of 7. In a tumor with a 3+3=6, the tumor is all pattern 3, and they are added together for a Gleason score of 6. Other ways that a Gleason score of 6 may be listed on your report are: "Gleason 6/10" or "Gleason 6 (3+3)" or "combined Gleason grade of 6".

5. *What does it mean to have a Gleason score of 6 or 7 or 8-10?*

The lowest Gleason score (least aggressive) tumor that is typically present on prostate biopsy is a 6 with higher grades (maximum Gleason score 10) corresponding to progressively more aggressive tumors.

6. *What does it mean when there are different cores with different Gleason scores?*

Different cores may sample different areas of the same tumor or different tumors in the prostate. Because the grade may vary within the same tumor or between different tumors, different samples taken from your prostate may have different Gleason scores. Typically the highest (largest number) Gleason score will be the one used by your doctor in predicting prognosis and deciding therapy.

7. *Does the Gleason score on my biopsy accurately indicate what the cancer grade is in the entire prostate?*

The Gleason score on biopsy is usually an accurate record of your cancer's true grade. However, in about 20% of cases the biopsy grade is lower than the true grade because the biopsy misses a higher grade (more aggressive) area of the tumor. In some cases, the biopsy grade can also overestimate the aggressiveness of the tumor, where the true grade of the tumor may be lower than what is seen on the biopsy.

8. *How important is the Gleason score? The Gleason score is one of the most powerful predictors of the behavior of prostate cancer but must be factored in with other information, such as the PSA blood test level, findings on rectal exam, number of cores involved by cancer, and in some cases radiology imaging studies to fully predict how the tumor will behave.*

According to my attending urologist, anything else would be too risky, like "watch and wait" or "radiation seeds". The fact that I was young enough to recover and "hopefully" restore my sexual function and continence (not peeing in my pants all the time or wearing a diaper) made this decision easier. "Of course, there are no guarantees", he continued on.

"Although I don't do prostate surgeries myself, I can assure you that my partner is highly skilled and successful at it and has even trained in Robotic surgery", the doctor stated. (Robotic surgery is supposed to be less invasive and spare the nerves that allow you to have an erection). He walked my wife and me around the corner to another office to meet his "partner doctor".

We sat in his office for about 20 minutes contemplating our decisions when the other doctor walked in. The first thing I noticed was he was about 70 years old. Strike One! I then proceeded to ask him just how many Robotic prostate surgeries he has performed. "About two or three a month" he boasted. Strike Two! Why do I want a guy that does 15 or 20 of these a year? I want the guy that's doing 15 a week! And a doctor that's not 70 years old. Odds are he didn't start doing these Robotic surgeries until three or four years ago. Now maybe I misread him or maybe I just didn't trust him. I knew I no longer trusted his partner since I felt that I had been walking around with prostate cancer now for over three years and he had not been able to diagnose me properly. Now my odds of this disease not spreading were extremely reduced.

I allowed their office to set up the mandatory pre-surgery testing. This includes a full CT scan of the lower abdomen with contrast dye. It also includes a nuclear bone scan since prostate cancer loves to travel to the bones. I went through the tests and waited extremely impatiently for the results of both. Days went by for the CT SCAN, but from the Bone Scan, (which I could view while they were performing it) they were able to tell me that no signs of metastatic disease existed. I finally got the all clear on the CT scan about 4 days later. Ok, now what do I do?

I have a close friend who happens to live down the block from me and went through prostate cancer surgery a couple of years before my diagnosis. I remember him telling me after the fact that he went to Johns Hopkins as that was where his wife found this doctor who was renowned for saving the nerves around the prostate that controls your ability to get an erection. This was the most important part to her. Curtis gave me the name and I called down to Johns Hopkins and made an appointment with this doctor. Curtis had good results but his wife still left him when his abilities did not come back right away and probably for a variety of other reasons. That's a nice caring wife. He was devastated and took him months if not years to get over it.

In the interim, I wasn't totally assured of this doctor at Johns Hopkins and the appointment was three weeks into the future. It was now early June. I kept doing my homework and researching my options.

I was discussing my situation with my older brother, Jeff. He has been in the medical staffing business for the past 20 years. He knew a lot of doctors and a lot about medicine in general. Unfortunately, Jeff and I have always been a little bit aloof because Jeff has some issues and tends to "enhance the truth" in many circumstances. Basically, you can't always trust him or what he promises.

Jeff said to me that "Dr. John Fueng who works out of Penn Medicine in Philadelphia is one of the best robotic prostate surgeons in the country." Ok, I'm listening. Jeff continued on that he "knows the main secretary and he would call her and that I should follow it up with a call and an Email the next day". Now I have to say, I had great trepidation that my dear brother Jeff was actually going to be able to help me.

I began to do some research on Dr. Fueng and to Jeff's point, he was extremely highly regarded. He was the guy teaching all of the other doctors how best to perform this procedure and how best to save the nerves around the prostate. He was so highly regarded that you normally would need to wait three months to get an appointment with him.

I followed Jeff's directives, emailed and then called to speak with his lead secretary. I pleaded my case to her and explained how I believed that I had this for almost three years and they just missed it with the first biopsy. You can "miss it" during biopsy because the prostate is a large acorn like organ and has four quadrants and if you take the sample from one of the areas and miss the cancer it will come back negative. In my case they missed it the first time altogether, but the second time it was actually present in two of the four quadrants. I continued that I had already had the bone scan and CT abdominal scan and that I could have those results emailed to Dr. Fueng at once.

She informed me that Dr. Fueng had "ONE OPENING" on Wednesday June 30th. I asked her if this was "for a consultation"? She said, "No, for Surgery" and that I would need pretesting by their hospital prior but that she would schedule me for surgery and I could come down the week earlier and do all of the pretesting. My appointment with the doctor at Johns Hopkins wasn't until July 1st. My wife and I discussed it and we just decided that we had a very competent and highly recommended surgeon who was willing to operate in 10 days on me and that was better than a trip to Maryland to see if we liked this doctor and who knows how long until I can get in for the actual surgery.

I knew deep down that I had this cancer for the past three years, even the during the time I was going through my breast cancer. I felt like I couldn't wait much longer as I was probably pushing my luck as it was going on for this long. I know the tests didn't show anything but I also knew that once the cancer reached the end of the capsule and could possibly escape into the blood stream, my chances of survival were considerably reduced.

It is widely known that prostate cancer is one of the more curable cancers, as long as you catch it early. But "if" and "when" it returns, prostate cancer is NOT curable at all. You can treat it with castration by drugs

(Lupron) or possible radiation, but "You Can Not Cure It". You may live 10 years or possibly a little longer once it returns, but eventually it will go to the bones and it will invade a vital organ and you are finished.

I wasn't going to wait. I accepted the appointment. I called my current Rochester, NY urologist and asked them to send all of my records along to Dr. Fueng's office. I drove down to Philly for a consultation and pre-testing with my surgical date already set for June 30th. The following week, my wife and I drove back down to Philly and checked into a nice hotel not far from the Penn Presbyterian hospital where the surgery was to be performed. I was nervous about the surgery only from the point of where the cancer had gone by now. I didn't really care about all of the possible side issues of incontinence or impotence. I couldn't go there. I already had one cancer that I felt like I was on the road to beating. Beating this one was all that mattered to me at this point.

The surgery is a bear of a surgery. They cut through layers and layers of your lower abdomen. Fortunately Dr. Fueng has a teaching video that I found a link to but I didn't watch it until "after the surgery" and while I was recuperating. It's very bloody and very tough to get to the prostate to remove it. I find it interesting that they can feel it easily with a rectal exam or even going through the rectal wall to biopsy it, but when it comes to the actual surgery, they cannot go in from that side because of the possibility of infection from the rectum and bowel.

They peel and peel away layer after layer all while attempting to avoid the pivotal nerves that control your urinary and erection functions. The "Robot" called "Da Vinci" actually has four arms so there are four incisions made so they can get at it from all sides. A fifth incision is made right above your belly button and in this hole a camera is inserted to guide them along.

Somehow, I / we got through the surgical part. My wife was accompanied by my sister Vicki for most of that day. I was the last case for Dr. Fueng on this Wednesday. I'm not sure if this was because he felt I was going to be the hardest case or because I was last to be scheduled. We waited in pre-op for what seemed like 10 hours. It was actually a little bit over three hours. The scheduling must have been a result of being in "sort of shape" because I was later informed that the overweight guys are the most difficult for them. There are more layers to cut through, so they operate on them first.

I awoke to the news that my surgery had gone well and that Dr. Fueng did everything he could to salvage my "important nerves" in the area. They would know more after the full pathology report. I had a catheter inserted (which has always been one of my greatest medical fears) while I was still under anesthesia and that I needed to come back to the office in six days to have the catheter removed.

Chapter 16
A SEINFELD EPISODE KIND OF A DAY:

Donna and I decided to stay in the Philadelphia area after I was discharged on Friday. I had to be back in five days and the five-plus hour drive home and back didn't exactly seem all that appealing. I wouldn't have to stop to go to the bathroom every two hours, which was my former normal, as I had this nice little contraption tube extending from my penis into a bag wrapped around my leg. My sister Vicki was nice enough to allow us to stay in her house while she and her family were "down the shore" in Margate for the July 4th weekend.

Vicki had offered us to come and stay with them "down the shore", but we didn't want to be a burden to them plus we would have had to displace one of their kids to take up a room. We retreated to her beautiful home in Harleysville, a northeastern suburb of Philadelphia and spent Friday there. A quick stop at Whole Foods to pick up some essentials and off we went.

It was kind of depressing. Here we were in this big house all alone. The weather was stifling hot, nearly 100 degrees every day. I was still hurting quite a bit from surgery and obviously couldn't do too much. I would have gone straight to the shore once Vicki invited us but Donna was very uncomfortable with the whole premise. By Friday evening, Donna started to feel as I did, that it was going to be a very long weekend alone in this strange house with 100 degree temperature outside. She agreed and I called Vicki and asked her if the offer was still open to come down to the shore house. "Of course" she said and we left very early on Saturday morning to beat the traffic and drove the 75 miles "to the Atlantic City suburb of Margate, down the shore".

It turned out to be a great idea. First it was 15-20 degrees cooler by the ocean. But it also allowed Donna some company to enjoy the holiday weekend. Of course I had to be careful as I couldn't get sand or ocean water into my incisions and we were still knocked out from the surgery and the stress. We laid low and tried not to infringe on my sister's holiday weekend with her family.

" My Little Sister Vicki and Me at her Margate, NJ Home"

On Tuesday morning we left early and drove back to Dr. Fueng's office in Philadelphia. As we walked into the offices, the scene was surreal. There were all of these guys sitting around the waiting room, mostly in shorts and a tee shirt with their catheter bags hanging out from beneath the bottom of their shorts. Dr. Fueng operates on Monday's and Wednesdays', usually five to seven cases on each day.

On the following Tuesday all of the 10-14 guys come back to the office for their follow up and to have their catheters removed.

One by one we would be called back. Most of the guys proceeded with extreme caution and trepidation. Most of us had never had a catheter removed and none of us were looking forward to it. As each guy went back Donna and I noticed that they would spend about 15 minutes or so and then come back out to the waiting area, but did not head out the door to leave.

At first, we weren't sure what was happening. They would go in to the exam area, come back out without "their friend, the catheter bag" and sit around a water cooler drinking large cup after large cup of water.

The rationale behind the water cooler extravaganza was that you had to be able to "pee" on your own before you were able to leave. The nurse would say that you have about 90 minutes to accomplish this or they would be forced to "re-insert" the catheter. NO ONE WANTED TO FIND OUT WHAT IT FELT LIKE TO HAVE SAID CATHETER REINSERTED WHILE THEY WERE AWAKE.

One by one they'd go in. One by one they'd come out, then drink and drink and drink to see if you could urinate on your own.

When the urge hit they would head back into the exam rooms, where the bathrooms were and after about three minutes come out with their hands raised over their head like they just won the heavyweight championship of the world!

"Rocky-esque"!

Pure jubilation!

Everyone else in the room would applaud and cheer their self-urination victory.

Removing the catheter wasn't as difficult as it seemed except that Dr. Fueng's nurse was a very pretty young lady. She instructs you to take a deep breath while lying flat on your back and then tells you to exhale completely. While exhaling... she basically yanks the tube right through your penis and it was all done. A little sore, but done.

Then... that ultimate first urination! Yes it was a joyous occasion knowing you weren't going to have to go back in and have the catheter re inserted. But what was it going to feel like? Would it hurt?

Well actually it burned like hell, which I kind of expected. After all I did have this rubber tube down there for almost a week now. What caught me off guard was the stream. I had spent the better part of the past three years fighting to get a good steady stream and completely empty my bladder. Suddenly, I had a "Fucking Firehouse" for a penis. It had such force that it was shooting all over the place.

WOW! Like I was 13 again!

Donna and I thought that this whole drama where all of these guys would wait to urinate and then celebrate would have made a great Seinfeld episode.

What we didn't account for was that once I was discharged we had the five and a half hour drive home to Rochester. I remember being ecstatic that I could pee again on my own and that this second cancer surgery in 18 months was behind me. I couldn't get out of there fast enough. Of course there was no full pathology report yet and I would need to return in a few weeks to have everything checked out and to hear about the "path report".

We scurried downstairs and retrieved our car and off we went for the five plus hour drive home.

What they didn't tell me was that all that water I drank in attempt to force my first urination on my own was about to cause one of the worst drives of my life. 15 minutes outside of downtown Philly and voila', I had to go. As I informed Donna who was driving, she said, "Ok, let's find a rest area". "NOPE" I replied, "I have to go... NOW!"

"Find a parking lot, a tree, I don't care, but find a place to stop because it's not going to wait".

They must have forgotten to tell us that part. I no longer had much, if any control and all that water added in made for about 10 "rest stops" over the next five hours. I was almost longing for that catheter bag.

Well, not quite... but almost.

Chapter 17

BREAST CANCER FOLLOW UP TIME:

It's Sunday August 9th. Tomorrow morning I have a 9:00 AM appointment with Dr. Miller, my breast cancer oncologist. It's been four months since my last follow up. This was the longest I have gone without visiting the University of Rochester Medical Center's Wilmot Cancer Center. A wonderful, brand new facility that I noticeably HAVE NOT MISSED.

It's a great facility but every time you walk into the hallway with the big sign overhead that reads; "Wilmot Cancer Center", your legs quiver a little. It's a harsh taste of realty that comes back and kicks you in the head because it reminds you that "you are and will always be... A Cancer Patient".

I find it very interesting that whenever I get into a discussion with a customer or stranger maybe on a plane and the conversation somehow leads to the fact that I am a cancer survivor the other person almost always says, "Congratulations".

At first I would wonder "why are they were congratulating me" like I had something to do with it?

But in fact I DID! At least I like to feel that I continue to have a major impact on my cancer and my health. The decisions I've made and the lifestyle choices I've changed over these past four years are significant and not always easy. The amounts of supplements I take and the organic food choices I make are expensive but nothing is too expensive, in my opinion, if it works and keeps me cancer free. I often heard pre-cancer about how you can mentally affect your cancer by being positive. I'm sure that has something to do with it and I certainly have tried but I feel it's a total package program. Your medical choices, your food and supplement decisions and especially your alcohol intake play major roles in keeping your immune system strong and being able to fight off any new cancer cells.

Ok I was here once over the past four months, but that was to visit Dr. Lee at the Department of Genetics. The doctor ordered my blood test designed to determine if I was a carrier of a genetic mutation that caused my getting breast cancer in the first place.

We talked about family history and the fact that my sister Vicki had been confirmed as a carrier for the BRCA 2 mutation gene. I checked in and the receptionist greeted me with the cordial expression, "How are you doing Mr. Singer". I never had to worry that the entire office wouldn't recognize me or treat me like "just another patient".

It's pretty easy to remember the one or two MALE PATIENTS who grace this facility on a regular basis. Shortly I was shuttled back to a small consultation office. Minutes later, Dr. Lee came in holding a few files in his hand. He was accompanied by a young female medical resident, who politely introduced herself as well. She was all wide-eyed and sponge like in her desire to learn. To learn more about this guy with breast cancer, I'm guessing.

We chatted casually and openly for a few minutes with the normal "how are you doing" type conversation among the three of us. Finally, Dr. Lee looked at me and opened his file.

He promptly blurted out, "Well, I guess we found out what we already knew? You are BRCA2 Positive"

DUH!

Doc proceeded to talk to me about all of the OTHER possibilities this mutation can cause. He said that prostate cancer and pancreatic cancer were two of the more evident ones. He wasn't making me feel any better about my situation.

He also began to talk to me about my lifestyle, especially going forward.

I explained to him that I have worked extremely hard since my chemo treatments on getting myself back in shape. I have been walking four to five miles, five to six times per week. These aren't casual strolls in the park either. Although they are in the park for the most part, as one mile away from my home I have the largest park in Monroe County, New York. Mendon Ponds Park.

As long as I'm home and not traveling for business, and weather permitting, I will find one hour of time during my day, don my IPOD and headphones, stretch a little and head out. My goal is to do the four and a half miles in under 55 minutes. I don't run because after my last meniscus surgery, a few years back, there's not much cartilage left in my right knee. The pounding of running hurts. I do walk at an extremely fast pace, and with the many hills in the park, this pace will induce a nice sweat and get my heart rate up.

While traveling on business I always attempt to get my workouts in, whether it is in the hotel's fitness center or if I'm in a warmer climate just a good 50-60 minute power walk.

I also explained that I have severely cut down my alcohol consumption.

Over the past four years, working as a Director of Sales in the hospitality industry, my job and travel have enticed me to drink more than I ever had in my life. Don't get me wrong, I was never angelic when it came to partying. But as a child of a big city, growing up in the 60's and 70's, my drug of choice was not necessarily alcohol. We had many other "choices" to pick from.

But my new career path allowed me to eat and drink for a living. One of my closest co-workers, Jeff, re-introduced me to Tequila four years earlier. Like most of us who partied our way through the 70's, just the smell of Tequila would cause a certain amount of nausea to overcome me. Ok a margarita I could handle, but straight Tequila, No Way!

Except that changed and changed quickly. Jeff introduced me to GOOD TEQUILA. The high end $60.00 to $100.00 bottles of Anejo's and good Reposado's that were aged two or more years. SMOOTH GOLD.

Within a year I became a connoisseur of fine tequilas. I knew them all and had tasted them all. There was nothing better than a Don Julio, Anejo poured NEAT, with a bottle of Perrier to chase it. No Garnish. No Salt. No Shots. Just smooth sipping tequila.

What I found out was that we all got sick from guzzling and having shots, of rat gut tequila. Bad tequila will make you sick and gave you the worst hangover imaginable. Good tequila, you can sip it all night, get a great Buzzzz and as long as you don't mix it with another alcoholic beverage, you will wake up fresh and ready to go the next morning.

While I was discussing how I've totally reduced my alcohol intake down to a minimum, Dr. Lee had a strange look on his face. He then proceeded to explain to me how the pancreas has to work exceptionally hard to filter out the alcohol I consume. BRCA2 also has the ability to cause pancreatic cancer so you don't want to tax it and make it more vulnerable.

For those who don't know, pancreatic cancer has one of the lowest survival rates for any of the cancers. I once discussed this at length with my gastro doctor as to why pancreatic cancer has such a low survival rate?

Dr. Greenfield, who has treated me for years for my colitis condition, was always open to discussions on these types of subjects. After one of my closest friends, Howard, lost his dad to pancreatic cancer, I asked Dr. Greenfield, "WHY DOES THIS HAVE SUCH A HIGH FATALITY RATE"? At that time, I had no idea I was carrying the BRCA 2 Gene, or anything else to do with me. It was because Howard's dad, Joe, a gem of a man lost his battle to pancreatic cancer as did his brother, cousin and aunt.

Dr. Greenfield explained to me that in all the years of his gastro-practice he had only had two people survive this dreaded disease. Both times they found the cancer while looking for something else and it was still early. It seems pancreatic cancer doesn't show (or present in medical lingo) any specific symptoms, and when it finally does, it's usually too late.

As I left the genetics office with a packet in hand describing my mutation, I began to contemplate where I was going with all of this new information. I knew I wasn't going to the liquor store!

By the time I arrived home some 20 minutes later I realized that tequila was no longer going to have a place in my life. In fact, most alcoholic beverages were about to be stricken from my diet. It just didn't seem worth it to me.

Most people don't realize that alcohol is a carcinogen. But it is! I'm not sure why nobody knows this or if it's a product of being such a mega billion dollar industry, which is heavily taxed, that it's swept under a rug somewhere. I just figured that I have so many other issues going on right now, I don't need to encourage these cancer cells to grow or for my already suspect pancreas to work harder.

Sure I miss being able to sit in a bar in Orlando or in New York City and nurse a good stiff drink. Sure I miss that "unwinding" that we all seem to need at day's end. Sure I miss the "Cart Girl" at The Mendon Golf Club bringing me that cold beer during a hot round of golf. Mostly I miss partaking in that perfect margarita I've learned to make for my wife on a lazy Saturday evening, even though I still make it for her.

But these are choices I have made and I have to live with "my" priorities. Believe me, I often think, "Why am I doing this? Why am I giving up these things when it possibly won't do me any good or potentially change what may or may not be growing in me?

I'm just trying to be able to live with the least amount of fear. It just seems that by drinking, when most physicians are saying it can aid in the recurrence of my breast cancer or cause my pancreas to work harder, I'm going to cause more fear to creep into my thoughts. I don't know exactly why but these are extremely hard decisions.

The exercise and alcohol non-consumption are just two small parts of what I am attempting to do for myself to help keep the cancers from returning or new cancers from forming.

I no longer purchase chicken or eggs that are not from organic or free range chickens. I eat very little beef or other red meats and if I do, I attempt to insure that they are from grass fed, antibiotic and hormone free animals. I drink very little milk, but if I do it is organic in nature.

I take a large amount of supplements that my brother in law and pharmacist Gary, has put together for me and ensure I keep to my daily schedule as best as possible. Some people think this is overkill and I often hear the skeptics questioning whether all that money and inconvenience is worth it.

My response is usually, "I don't know if it works or if it's worth it? I just know that IF IT KEEPS THE CANCER AWAY, IT'S WORTH EVERY PENNY AND EVERY MINUTE OF MY TIME!"

Today I will meet with Dr. Miller. It's been four months and I have no idea what happens next to me. I know that I feel like I'm in shape and although I have the 55 year old aches and pains, they seem fairly normal. I'm playing golf at least twice a week, walking the course every time. The days I walk 18, I usually don't do my four or five miles, but sometimes I will if Donna wants to walk as well. It has taken me a few months to gain back the ability to swing a club as the left side they cut open has had some residual pain areas. I've never been a great golfer. Hell, I've never even been a good golfer. But I love to play. I love the fact that when I'm out on the course there's so much "golf stress" that I can use that four plus hours to not think about my disease or any of the other possibilities from it. There's enough thought needed to keep my swing on plane, keep my head down and to follow through.

We'll see what tests or procedures come next, hopefully nothing too significant or too painful. I now that they want to monitor the "other" side. I know they want me to have mammograms and MRI's regularly to ensure there's nothing new forming. Many times I think to myself, WHY DIDN'T I HAVE BOTH SIDES REMOVED DURING THE SURGERY? Bilateral as they call it. I just wasn't prepared to make that decision at the time and I wanted to schedule the surgery as soon as possible. As long as I pay attention to my body and continue to be watched closely, I feel I can catch any new breast cancers early on.

I've thought about having the right side done and possibly having reconstruction of both sides to give me back my "male definition". But the thought of more surgery and more possible complications, at this time at least, just doesn't entice me. But I am still considering it.

Up to date, I do have annual MRI's and alternating six month mammograms. I do annual contrast CT's of my lower abdomen. Recently I had a new test called an endoscopic ultrasound. The endoscope goes down through the mouth and throat and with an ultrasound camera on the other end and they are able to scan the pancreas. I plan on doing these annually going forward.

With my prostate cancer I'm monitored every three to four months with new PSA tests. My PSA needs to remain below 0.08 or undetectable. Any PSA of measureable amount will indicate that my prostate cancer is surfacing somewhere else. My erectile function has returned to about 80% of my normal, mostly with the help of those wonderful E.D. Drugs. My continence is doing well as I continue to do my "Kegel" exercises.

I just keep working on all aspects and hoping beyond hope that I have no recurrences.

Cancer does amazing things to you and your mind. You can never really get too comfortable that things are under control. I marvel at those who can just put it to the side and go on living their lives. I guess it takes a certain type of personality or mindset, one that I obviously don't have.

It also changes things and alters your prior fears. For example I fly a lot for business. I have spent the better part of the past 35 years flying at least once or twice a month on business or sometimes for vacation. As much of a "seasoned flier" as I was, I still had a terrible fear, mostly on take-offs when a majority of air travel accidents occur. I would literally get sweaty palms and go through superstitious routines during every take-off.

Amazingly, immediately after my cancer surgery and when I began to travel again, I no longer had any fear of flying! It was crazy but it was totally gone from my being and my mind. It was almost like, "fine, if I have to go, let it be this way". I don't know why it happened this way, I just know that it did and it's was definitely just another example of how cancer can affect everything in your life.

Chapter 18

HIS BREAST CANCER AWARENESS FOUNDATION:

While I was going through chemo for my breast cancer, I had some extra time on my plate. I worked as much as possible and thankfully the understanding owners of my company worked with me throughout the process. This time allowed me to first begin the authoring of these pages. My goal was not to write some New York Times best seller but was rather to keep my mind occupied and allow me the outlet to express myself, my feelings and my fears.

The second and more important thing that happened to me during Chemo-Hell was that I was able to realize how frustrating and how awful the process was for a **"Guy going through a Woman's Disease"**. The total lack of accurate information, accompanied by the embarrassment and humiliation, on top of dealing with normal cancer issues, definitely got to me.

The embarrassment and humiliation came from a variety of sources. First you have the early on procedures which include "mammograms". The filling out of the paperwork each and every time you enter the imaging center is always troubling. I believe that most of these places change their medical secretary's on a regular basis. This causes the newest "check in girl" to always stumble and do some double takes when I arrive for my mammogram.

Inevitably it requires the forms to be completed with large breasted women on the diagrams and those questions that pertain to things like menopause and recent PAP smears in addition to normal medical information.

My golf buddies for the first year always asked me "if I preferred to play from the red tees?" (The red tees are designed for the women players). Actually for about the first 18 months post surgery I lost about 30 yards off my driver and all of my irons needed to increase to help with the distance. This was probably because my "left side" had so much tissue loss and scarring from my mastectomy or maybe it was just because I hadn't played in a while and was tentative. Either way, it made for some snide comments from the rest of the foursome.

As we walked our 18 holes we would talk about many things but inevitably it would circle back to my cancer and condition even if was just to ask me how I was doing.

My closest friends, the guys in the "Philly Boyz" group, began to refer to me as O.T. One guy, I think it was Murray, started calling me that in one Email chain and it stuck. O.T. stands for **"One Tit"**. Now every Email and verbal conversation refers to me as O.T. I choose to believe it's a term of endearment. I wonder if I chose to have Bi-Lateral Mastectomy if they would call me N.T. for no tits?

The reaction when you speak to people and you discuss the fact that you're a **"Man with Breast Cancer"** is usually one where they either show disbelief or one where they attempt to act like they knew a lot about the facts. More often it is "I didn't know men could get breast cancer?"

When I arrive for any check up with my oncologists whether it's my breast or for my prostate, I have to be examined by one to three residents. They all want to do an exam and learn about my case, since it's rare to have a guy with this disease. I am very amenable to their plight and education, really to my plight as well, which is to bring more awareness and knowledge to the men fighting breast cancer.

I promised myself that IF and WHEN I beat this thing I would find a way to help the next guy to not have to deal with all the things that I went through.

Between Vicki and me we have five boys. All of our kids are in their late 20's to early 30's. We have no girls. Because Vicki and I are BRCA 2, the mutation that caused our breast cancer, the odds are 50/50 that each of our sons could also be carrying the BRCA 2 mutation. We talked throughout my process of finding a way to reach the other guys. We know they are out there, but most are too embarrassed to want to discuss their disease.

I have never had any problem talking about my breast cancer. I would talk to anyone who would listen and besides a little ribbing from my close friends and golf buddies, I never once felt uncomfortable talking about it. I did feel uncomfortable for the first couple of years when visiting our favorite beaches in St. Maarten or in Atlantic City or even poolside when on some business trips, with regard to my disfigured chest area. I could have had reconstruction and maybe even look a little younger and more "cut", but I never chose to go that route. After a while I would actually look for people to question my "one-tit" appearance and even if they didn't say anything to me and I knew they were noticing it, I would engage the conversation with them.

The reason I have been able to survive this so far is because it was caught fairly early before any lymph node involvement or metastasis. **Men need to know that they can get breast cancer and that they can DIE from it!**
They Don't!

Vicki and I went to work on finding a way to reach the men out there. We needed a way to get the insurance companies to change their rules and allow men (like our sons) who are at higher risk, to be screened. Women can get annual mammograms. Why can't our sons who may be at a higher risk get one annually as well? It just doesn't make any sense.

We decided to attempt to form a foundation for **"Male Breast Cancer Awareness"**. Believe me it was and still is not a mainstream topic. The NFL for instance spends millions of dollars every October promoting "Breast Cancer Awareness" and never once do they ever mention anything about guys.

Last season, 2012, for the first time I actually saw a story on one of the Philadelphia Eagles whose father was a breast cancer survivor. Vicki lives in Philadelphia and I am a rabid fan of the Eagles. We both spent countless hours attempting to reach Kurt Coleman by Email, Twitter and even through the Eagles public relations office. He would not return any contact attempts nor come close to discussing it with us.

On a vacation in the winter of 2012 to St. Maarten, I ran into Dan Patrick from NBC Sports and the Dan Patrick Show. We met while waiting for the baggage to come down from the plane on the Island. Dan and his entire family were on a last minute trip to St. Maarten when some other plans were forced to change. Donna and I have been to St. Maarten about seven times before this trip and we know the Island very well, including all of the best restaurants.

Dan had never been to St. Maarten and had little time to research it. He was very interested in my suggestions for dinners and beaches. I actually gave him quite a few of our regular stops.

Ironically we ended up seeing Dan and his family multiple times throughout the week at most of the places I suggested for dinner. After the fourth chance meeting I decided to see if I could bridge the topic of HIS BREAST CANCER AWARENESS FOUNDATION to him, not for his money, but for him to help us the following October during Breast Cancer Awareness Month. This would bring the topic of Male Breast Cancer to light. His show reaches a million men daily and it seemed like an opportune way to assist us.

He immediately pushed back and wanted "nothing" to do with me or our foundation from that point forward. I guess he just didn't feel comfortable talking about male breast cancer. This was not that unusual as most guys will hesitate to discuss this topic.

As we found out quickly this was not an easy process. We had to file and re file all of the paperwork allowing us to form a "Not-for-Profit" organization under the laws of the United States, the IRS and the state of New York. We are a fully recognized 501C Exempt organization. Luckily we have quite a few friends in the legal and in the accounting business who were able to assist us.

We needed a name for this organization.

As I referenced early on in these pages, I never liked my first name or my middle name. "Harvey Irwin" was not at the top of "the cool names list". What I did always think was cool during my youth was the fact that my initials spelled out "HIS".

It became fairly evident to me and Vicki that HIS BREAST CAN-CER AWARENESS would take on a dual meaning. "His" meaning for him or about him and "H.I.S.", being my initials made up the perfect combination.

HIS BREAST CANCER AWARENESS FOUNDATION was formed.

It has taken us the past several years just to get some recognition. The year 2012 was a banner year for our foundation as we were able to partner with some other organizations and find some large benefactors.

FORCE (Facing Our Risk of Cancer Empowered) is an amazing orga-nization for "Previvors". Previvors is a coined term for those people who are at a high risk for cancer, like BRCA positive or for any of those with a strong family history of cancer. They do a great job and we were able to publicize *HIS* **Breast Cancer Awareness Foundation** through their National convention in Orlando. We're hopeful with a few more dollars raised this coming year, that we can actually have a booth at their conven-tion in the future.

Championship Billiard Cloth, who is a leading company in the bil-liards supply business, approached us about doing a major awareness fundraiser during October 2012. Championship created a package that included a pink rack, pink cushion, pink & blue chalk and a "cue ball with the *HIS Logo* on it". They sold these packages to many of their billiard hall customers as well as other suppliers. Because the billiard business is male dominated, they wanted to work with us rather than with some of the mainstream breast cancer foundations like Susan G. Komen.

Championship Billiard Cloth raised and donated thousands of dollars for our cause.

HIS realized that we could not discuss anything medically with any of the men that find us from around the world. We actually get emails to our website from guys all over the U.S. and from as far away as Australia, who are looking for someone to talk to, someone to just listen to them.

We have four prominent medical advisors on our board to verify our information on an ongoing basis and to insure its accuracy.

Just a few weeks ago my surgeon referred a gentleman to me and our **HIS Foundation** as he had just completed having his left breast removed in a complete mastectomy. He contacted us through our site and Vicki referred the contact to me. I sent him an email and then spent about 90 minutes on the phone with his wife and him.

His case was a lot more involved than mine as he was diagnosed at the time of surgery with a Stage "3" Cancer and had 29 lymph nodes removed during surgery as well. He is facing about 12-15 months of chemo and radiation. What caught my attention was that during our discussion he told me that he first noticed some changes in his left breast about 10 years before his diagnosis. He made several subsequent trips to his personal physician to discuss his symptoms and was told multiple times that "it was nothing".

Being a guy, like most guys, he took the doctor at his words. Not once did the doctor order a mammogram or choose to look further. He told me that it wasn't until this past summer during a boating outing that his friend noticed that his left breast "looked swollen". At this point he took the problem more seriously and finally insisted that they find the root cause of the swelling and pain.

Male Breast Cancer!

It took them 10 years to diagnose it.

With more awareness and public knowledge and even more detailed activity among the medical community this would have and should have been caught years earlier. Subsequently, this would have enabled him to have a much easier road into beating the disease.

Another gentleman I spoke with about three months prior to this one, also went through surgery and was scheduled for chemo. We caught up while he and his wife were taking a long drive through the Finger Lakes area of Upstate, NY. At the end of the conversation he thanked me over and over for giving them so much time and assisting him. What he didn't realize was that my conversation with him as well as with many others has a therapeutic effect on me as well.

I've always felt that if **I could help save ONE GUY from all the STRESS that I went through, "HIS Breast Cancer Awareness Foundation"** would be worth all of the work.

We chatted about all things including the preventative measures of diet and exercise that Vicki and I adhere to as best as possible. We choose to only drink organic milk, and only eat organic eggs. We make sure that the chicken, beef or any other meat products we ingest are never treated with hormones. Farmers use hormones added to the feed of the chickens and cows to "increase the yield" and grow the animals bigger or allow them to put out more eggs and milk. Breast cancer is a hormonally driven disease. The cancer cells thrive and reproduce with progesterone and estrogen. This is why most breast cancer patients take Tamoxifen. Tamoxifen tricks the cells into thinking they have enough of these hormones and they starve and die off.

Vicki and I only use deodorants that do not contain any aluminum. Putting aluminum under your arms can directly infect your lymph system and cause breast cancer cells to grow.

We attempt to hit the gym or do outside activities like walking or biking and get at least an hour or 90 minutes of good cardio exercise, four to five times per week. We take a regimen of vitamins and supplements that include Vitamin D and Vitamin C along with a wide variety of immune builders. Additionally we believe in things like eating plenty of leafy greens like kale, broccoli and Brussels sprouts. Turmeric and resveratrol are also extremely powerful cancer fighter supplements.

Sugar is the ultimate enemy of your immune system and this includes any white flour, pasta or potatoes that will turn the carbohydrates into sugar as it dissolves in your system. You can utilize whole grains (like whole wheat bread) or whole wheat pasta to replace the white flours. You can use sweet potatoes or yams instead of white potatoes.

Much about alcohol has been discussed in previous chapters and in the area of cancer in general. The jury is still out but there seems to be a definitive link between alcohol intake and cancer formation or reformation. I personally believe that much of the alcohol talk is related to the "sugar" talk as alcohol also becomes sugar to your system.

We had a former CFO at my company named Leon Constantainer. Leon was born and raised in Mexico was a fairly heavy smoker and very heavy Scotch consumer. About six months prior to my diagnosis, Leon was diagnosed with "tongue cancer". He had a few surgeries and fought as hard as anyone could fight to beat his disease. He resigned his position to go back to Boston where his wife was living and to be treated at the Dana Farber Cancer Hospital.

After about nine months of hell and after my diagnosis, Leon and I had dinner while out at our San Diego office. I remember Leon telling me that one of the first things his doctors told him was that alcohol of any variety was no longer a good option for him. Of course smoking was off the table as well. Leon said to me: "I'm going to do everything my doctor tells me because all I want to do is beat this thing and live."

Three months later, Leon's cancer came back and even though he was following all of the regimens set forth by "his doctor" and all of the initiatives at Dana Farber his outlook was not good. He kept up the fight from his Boston residence and I would visit him pretty much every time I got to Boston. Each visit he looked worse than he did the visit before.

Leon passed away in the summer of 2011. I have no hard evidence of this but I assume that his life- long heavy drinking and smoking most likely contributed to his demise.

If you want to reduce your sugar and choose to go to some of the more common sugar substitutes on the market like Equal or Splenda we suggest you look to Stevia. Stevia is now readily available as a viable and natural Non-Calorie sweetener. If you don't care about the calories, there is always "Agave". Agave is the natural sweetener that is extracted from the Agave plant. (Yes, the same one that forms TEQUILA). I guess it's ok to use a sugar substitute but not to drink tequila! There is a ton of sugar in most margarita mixes as well as in sour mix or Pina-Colada mix. Look at the labels for all sugar content for most of the products you buy. You'll be amazed how much sugar we're ingesting or giving our children.

Beer is a double whammy since its alcohol and made from grain. Both are negatives to your long term prognosis.

HIS Breast Cancer Awareness Foundation is a Non-Profit Organization designed to educate and inform for all things related to Male Breast Cancer. You can find **HIS Breast Cancer Awareness Foundation** on the web at WWW.HISBREASTCANCER.ORG.

Vicki and I, with the help of her two sons who have set up and monitor our website, will continue to do our life's work. We know how important it is to all of those men out there and their families. We know we have a lot of work to do and we can only accomplish what we want to do with the help of donations and other supporters.

People say that all things happen for a reason. I've never really subscribed to that theory, but so much along my journey seems to back this up. Why was I chosen to have this disease? I don't know, just maybe, it was because I was the one who chose to "do something about it".

We are hoping we can make this topic just a little bit more mainstream and help other men avoid the embarrassment and humility of being a **"Man with a Women's Disease"**.

If we can make the insurance companies come to grip with the fact that men at high risk, like our five sons, can get annual screening covered, like every woman does, it will be worth it!

If we can get a National movement to have the Third Week of October (Breast Cancer Awareness Month) to be "Male Breast Cancer Week", we know that our plight will become easier. Currently only four states recognize Male Breast Cancer Week. PA, NJ, FL and MA are the four states. Only 46 more states to go!

I started this book to keep my mind occupied during chemo. It is so much more important now than it was then. This book is a way to tell my story and enlighten others. I'm also hopeful that the proceeds will help us make this topic more mainstream and help us fund our **"HIS Breast Cancer Awareness Foundation"**. **100% of any proceeds from "Sir, You Have Breast Cancer" will go directly to our foundation.**

My goal and the goal of Vicki and our Foundation, **HIS BREAST CANCER AWARENESS**, is to help educate and inform that Male Breast Cancer does exist and that men can and will die from it.

We seek to make the topic of male breast cancer no longer a stigma, nor an embarrassment, that burdens so many men. We will work the rest of our days to make men aware that they can get this disease and that they can die from it, but that they don't have to.

My goal was always "**if I can save one guy's life**" it will all be worth-while. I think we have already done so much more and we will continue to work hard until we can make every man, plus every woman and child who loves him, aware that this disease is possible for guys as well.

Chapter 19
HARVEY'S PERFECT MARGARITA:

O k, I know I have preached to limit alcohol consumption, but I did develop the "Harvey's Perfect Margarita". I promised earlier to share the recipe:

Three Parts- Good Reposado Tequila plus
Two Parts-Yukon Jack (sweet Canadian Liquor) plus
One Part Cointreau (triple –sec)
Add in a ½ of a freshly squeezed Lime
Then equal the total volume with sour mix. (there are many Low Calorie or ½ the sugar, sour mixes on the market)
Add lots of Ice and a ½ cup of Fresh Squeezed Tangerine Juice. Shake vigorously for two to three minutes. No salt needed on the rim of the glass. Garnish with a lime skin.
PERFECT and POTENT! (Yukon Jack is 100% Proof, please drink responsibly!)

HARVEY'S FAMOUS GUACAMOLE:

Chop up finely about 1/4-1/3 of a sweet Onion. (Vidalia if in Season)
Cut up and remove the insides of Three Firm Plum Tomatoes. Chop the remaining tomato skins as small as possible

Chop up about 2/3 cup of fresh cilantro

Take two to three Haas Avocado's that are slightly firm but indent a little upon pushing with your finger.

Split the Avocados vertically, exposing the large middle pit. Remove the pit (by using a sharp heavy knife right across the middle and it should easily come out).

Using a 2 ½ inch paring knife, cut each of the avocado half's both vertically and horizontal, forming as small as possible, squares.

Scoop out the avocado from their half shells and place in a large bowl. Then add the chopped onions, tomatoes, and cilantro. Add a quarter of a teaspoon of Pepper and Kosher Salt.

Add a splash of lime juice.

Add 1/6 – 1/4 cup of fresh red hot chili peppers or use Nature's Squeeze Sweet Chili Pepper paste.

Mix but not too hard or long as you want to keep the avocado pieces in tack. Garnish with some lime on top.

You can serve this with cut up celery or cut up carrots, but of course most people prefer tortilla chips.

ENJOY!

ACKNOWLEDGMENTS:

MY Family: Donna, Harvey, Matthew & Jameson (2012)

There are many people in my life I need to thank, but none more important and foremost than my wife of 33 years, Donna. She was the rock I had to lean on and sat beside me on all of those horrible days and through all the tests and treatments. She never showed me any fear or panic and was always the calming influence. "We'll get through this" she would always remind me. "We will get through it!" I know now that without her, I never would have gotten through it!

Next is my sister Vicki, who has beaten breast cancer four times and was always upbeat and met the disease head on. She never wavered or gave in to it. She was my educator and guidance counselor and helped with many of my critical decisions. You can blame cancer for many things but I will thank cancer for bringing Vicki and I so close together. These pages have told how Vicki and I, in some ways, have cancer to be thankful for.

I have had so many great doctors and few not so great ones but I know they are all working so hard to help each and every patient survive and prosper.

My personal thanks to my attending breast oncologist, my urologic oncologist and my gastro (G.I.) Doctor who are among the most caring individuals I have ever met. To all of the amazing PA's and Nurses at Strong Memorial Hospital and the University of Rochester Medical Center, keep pushing forward because you all are the best. You help each and every cancer patient and do so with such grace and friendship.

I would have never completed these pages without the "push" and the care from my therapist. As my mental care doctor who managed to stabilize and encourage me when I started to go over the side of that mental cliff that so many cancer patients reach. A big Thank you!

To my boys Matthew and Jameson, for growing up to be such great "men" and for their understanding during all the hard times and a better understanding for their potential risks going forward. They know how much it hurts me to have them possibly living with the same BRCA mutation. Hopefully I have taught them enough to be **<u>Very Aware</u>** of their bodies. I LOVE YOU BOTH DEARLY!

To my Philly Boyz: All of you know how much your friendships mean to me and now you know how important you were as I undertook these large battles in my life. I so look forward to having us all together again this fall.

And last but certainly not least to my Mom, Libby who along with her 97 year old sister, my God-Mother, Aunt Ruth, have both survived breast cancer and so many other personal traumas in their lifetime. They handle it all with such grace and determination. They are truly an inspiration!

A special acknowledgment to Fred Grossman (cousin Fred): You helped me by being the first person who I allowed to read this original manuscript and you kept pushing me forward telling me how great a story it was and how important it was for me to complete it. Thank you very much!

Made in the USA
Middletown, DE
13 June 2019